The History of Marriage and Divorce

The History of Marriage and Divorce

Everything You Need to Know

HARRY L. MUNSINGER, J.D., PH.D.

Archway Publishing books may be ordered through booksellers or by contacting:

Archway Publishing
1663 Liberty Drive
Bloomington, IN 47403
www.archwaypublishing.com
1 (888) 242-5904

ISBN: 978-1-4808-8213-3 (sc)
ISBN: 978-1-4808-8212-6 (e)

Library of Congress Control Number: 2019913038

Print information available on the last page.

Archway Publishing rev. date: 9/10/2019

Contents

Chapter 1

The Goals of Marriage and Divorce

The goals of marriage include sex, financial support, social status, political connections, emotional fulfillment, personal attachment, romantic love, procreation, child-rearing, companionship, and inheritance rights. The goals of divorce involve dissolving a broken marriage, dividing assets, arranging spousal and child support, and planning custody and access to children. Marriage rituals and divorce procedures have varied widely over time and among cultures, but some system of pair-bonding has existed throughout human history in all known cultures except the Na people of China.[1]

Anthropologists and historians have found evidence of mated and single parents among ancient hunter-gatherer tribes, primitive groups living in remote areas of the modern world, and almost all ancient and modern civilizations. Ancient hunter-gatherer tribes had no known formal marriage system, but later societies generally developed formal social, religious, or legal systems that controlled and verified marriage and divorce.

There are two main patterns of marriage: monogamy and polygamy.

Monogamy and Polygamy

The most common pattern of marriage is serial monogamy, whereby couples marry, produce children, divorce, remarry, and produce more children.[2] Among the few societies where divorce is forbidden, marriages are annulled, legal separations are granted, and couples informally desert broken marriages and form new relationships.

The major alternative to serial monogamy is polygamy, whereby individuals marry several spouses. Polygamy is legal in many countries, but generally only rich men take advantage of the option, while most men and women marry one spouse or stay single.

Arranged Marriages

Historically, most marriages were arranged by the family.

For centuries, most marriages were arranged by families to meet economic, social, or political goals rather than for romantic love. In contrast, most modern marriages are based on romantic love.[3] These modern marriages are breaking up at an alarming rate, and conservative authorities worry that the institutions of marriage and family are being damaged by the high incidence of divorce. Critics believe that premarital sex, impersonal sexual hookups, trial marriages, cohabitation, same-sex marriages, and children born to single mothers show that traditional marriage is changing—and not for the better. Earlier generations expected most adults to marry, husbands to work, and wives to manage the home and raise the children. A generation ago, around 85 percent of Western women married, while today only about 50 percent of Western women under thirty-five years of age are married.[4] Many women are having children out of wedlock.

Marriage and reproduction are becoming independent events in many countries.[5] More than 40 percent of children in America are born to single mothers, while 60 percent of French children are born to unwed women. Studies show that children are developmentally disadvantaged when they lack two parents in the home. Marriage and reproductive patterns are more traditional in Asian and Middle Eastern countries. In Japan, for example, 2 percent of births occur among unmarried women. India and China also have low rates of births to unmarried parents.

Over the last fifty years, four major changes have occurred in the way people marry and divorce: who controls the marriage decision, the purpose of marriage, civil unions, and no-fault divorce. For generations, families arranged their children's marriages based on economic, social, and political considerations. Pretty young girls were married to wealthy men who could bring social status, riches, and power to the bride and her family. Today most marriages are agreed upon by the parties themselves, and couples are marrying later in life or not at all. The median age of marriage for women in America is now over thirty years. In earlier generations, women were usually married by twenty years of age.[6] Fewer persons are marrying these days because they are cohabiting or forming civil unions instead. Civil unions confer some of the rights and responsibilities of marriage and were originally intended as an alternative to same-sex marriage. Today heterosexual couples are forming civil-union partnerships rather than getting married, because they prefer not to make the commitments marriage demands, even though there are health and economic advantages to being married.

Benefits of Marriage

Numerous studies show that married couples are healthier, wealthier, and happier than single or divorced individuals.[7] However, until recently it wasn't known whether this positive effect was caused by being married or because healthy, wealthy, and happy individuals marry more often than sick, poor, and unhappy people do. To answer this question, researchers statistically controlled for the health, economic status, and psychological well-being of married spouses. They still found a significant benefit to being married. These results indicate that being married has a positive effect on health, wealth, and happiness independent of the fact that healthy, wealthy, and happy people marry more often.

Mate selection is also changing. In previous generations, it was common for individuals to marry a first cousin or other close family member. Charles Darwin married a first cousin and later lamented that inbreeding created evil effects among his children.[8] Today marriages between close relatives are rare, because most countries discourage them. Also, fewer people marry cousins today because lower birthrates are limiting the availability of first cousins as potential mates. When women had an average of five surviving children, females could expect to have around twenty-five male cousins. However, when the average birthrate is under two, females can expect to have only three or four male cousins, making it much less likely a consanguineous marriage can happen.

Modern individuals are selecting mates with similar educational attainment, social status, and personal values. Couples who marry the right person report their union produces happiness and emotional fulfillment, while unlucky couples report that marriage is a disappointment and they are unhappy with their mates. Significantly fewer couples are tying the knot these days, and of those who do, approximately 45 percent divorce at least once during their lives. Among couples who remarry after a divorce, the second and third marriages are even more likely to fail. And highly educated women are less likely to marry, stay married, or produce children.

Fewer Chinese Women

A unique marital problem is happening in China today because of an earlier government policy of allowing only one child per family.[9]

Because of the one-child policy enforced throughout China for more than a generation, many poor Chinese males are unable to find mates. Asian families generally prefer male offspring, so when families were restricted to one child, many couples aborted female fetuses, abandoned female babies, or placed them for foreign adoption and waited for a male child. An unintended consequence of this policy is that a significant number of young Chinese men have little chance of marrying, because there are too few females in their age group.

Under natural conditions, approximately 105 males are born for every 100 females. Because of higher natural attrition among young males, by the time these children become adults, the sex ratio is approximately 100 males for every 100 females. In China today, because of the one-child policy and the preference of Chinese families for male offspring, the sex ratio is approximately 115 young adult males for every 100 young adult females. This means young Chinese females can marry better-educated and wealthier males than they previously could, while many poor and uneducated Chinese males have difficulty finding mates. Desperate Chinese families are importing women from other countries for their sons to marry.

Another modern problem is that many children are being raised in single-parent homes, which has negative consequences for children.

Divorce and Children

We know that children, and especially boys, are adversely affected by a parental conflict associated with a divorce. Studies show that being raised in a single-parent household is associated with developmental problems, whether the single-parent home was created by divorce or out-of-wedlock childbirth.[10] Growing up with only one parent damages children, and this is particularly true when the parents' divorce was adversarial and created significant conflict. Children raised by one parent are more likely to be delinquent, drop out of school, use drugs, and experience emotional problems compared with children raised in a two-parent home.

But is this better outcome for children from intact families the result of having two parents in the home or because better-educated, richer, and happier couples stay married? To answer this question, researchers statistically controlled for education, wealth, happiness, and age differences between married and single households with children. They found that having married parents in the home confers a benefit on children compared with having divorced parents or living in a single-parent home. Having two parents in the home is better for children than being raised in a single-parent home, whether the single-parent status is caused by divorce or having a child out of wedlock. These results also suggest that better educated, wealthier, and happier single parents raise better-adjusted children than poor, unhappy, uneducated single parents.

Forming a Stable Marriage

Economists David Gale and Lloyd Shapley proposed a mathematical solution to forming stable marriages.[11] They asked men and women to rank their preferences for mates and then had men propose to their first choice. Women were told to keep the proposal from the man they preferred and reject all other marriage proposals in this first round. Each woman was also advised not to accept the first offer of marriage unless the man was the top-ranked mate on her list, because a higher-ranking male might propose later. Any man who was rejected by his first female choice was asked to propose to the second-ranked female on his list of available mates. Women again retained the proposal they preferred in this second round and rejected other marriage offers. The mating procedure was continued until all males were paired with the highest-preferred female who accepted them.

This may not be the most romantic process, but it's guaranteed to mate every male with the highest-ranked female who will accept his proposal. Females are at a modest disadvantage under this system; they might fare better if they could propose to males instead of having to wait for marriage proposals. This is because some males might not propose to highly desirable females, fearing they would be rejected. This procedure has a certain appeal to those who believe everyone should be married.

However, there's a flaw in this mating system. The economists assumed human preferences don't change, while we know they do. Relatively stable marriages form using this procedure, but people are living longer, and they change their preferences, get divorced, go through the marriage selection process again, and form another relationship based on their new marriage preferences. This process creates the typical pattern of serial monogamy. We have seen that the institution of marriage has changed over the last several generations. What about divorce—has it evolved as well?

Purpose of Divorce

The purpose of divorce is to separate couples whose marriages have broken down, divide their assets, and develop a parenting plan to nurture and support their children. Experts believe that early hunter-gatherer tribes encouraged couples to mate and allowed them to separate, so long as their children were protected. Among ancient civilizations such as those in Mesopotamia, Israel, Greece, and the Roman Empire, divorce was generally available to couples whose marriages were broken. Either the husband or wife could initiate divorce in many of these ancient societies. Early Mesopotamian, Jewish, and Greek civilizations allowed divorce for adultery, desertion, or barrenness, and Roman citizens needed no reason at all to divorce. After the Catholic Church became the state religion of

Rome, divorce and remarriage were gradually restricted and then forbidden. It was not until the Protestant Reformation during the sixteenth century that divorce again became available in Western Europe.[12]

Under ancient Catholic law, annulments could be purchased by wealthy or powerful families who wanted to terminate a marriage. The fee for an annulment is lower today, but Catholic doctrine still discourages divorce. Some Catholics divorce anyway.

Divorce Patterns

A striking feature of modern societies is how easy it is to dissolve a marriage. Luxembourg has the world's highest divorce rate at 87 percent, followed by Spain at 65 percent, France at 55 percent, Russia at 51 percent, and the United States at 46 percent. India has the world's lowest divorce rate at just over 1 percent. The average global divorce rate has increased from 12 to 44 percent in the last sixty years.[13] Despite the fact that marriage experts decry the high divorce rate among modern societies and warn that the institution of marriage may be on the verge of collapse, there is little support for repealing no-fault divorce laws. Moreover, it can be argued that the institution of marriage is alive and well, given the high rate of remarriage among divorced individuals.

What can be done to avoid the negative effects of divorce on parents and children? Should we make marriage dissolution more difficult, try to save marriages by requiring couples to enter counseling before filing for divorce, advise couples to postpone having children until their marriage appears stable, or advise couples to postpone divorce until their children are adults? Should we change the way we divorce in America? Is an adversarial divorce best?

Adversarial Divorce

The adversarial divorce process involves impartial judges, formal procedural rules, and attorneys who zealously represents the interests of their clients and attack the credibility of witnesses and evidence offered by opponents. The adversarial system underlies the entire American legal system and has a long history.[14] Before the Norman Conquest of England in 1066, Anglo-Saxon judicial procedures relied on God to determine the guilt or innocence of individuals brought before a tribunal. Saxon procedures for determining guilt or innocence relied on various forms of trial by battle.[15]

Trial by combat was a fight, often to the death, between the accused (or his champion) and the king's champion. If the accused survived or his champion won, the individual was presumed innocent. *Trial by ordeal* involved subjecting the accused person to a dangerous situation, such as immersion in water while bound hand and foot. If the accused survived, it was assumed God had intervened to save him or her, and that proved the person was innocent. Trial by ordeal is found in ancient Indian writings, in the Code of Hammurabi of ancient Mesopotamia, and in the Book of Numbers from the Old Testament, where Moses subjected a woman accused of adultery to this type of trial.

In *trial by compurgation*, the accused person's credibility was tested by having him or her recite a sworn oath of innocence. If a compurgator could recite the oath without mistakes, it was deemed valid, and the accused was set free. God was expected to intervene and determine whether the compurgator recited the oath accurately. It was assumed that God would twist a lying compurgator's tongue so he or she would make a mistake in reciting the oath of innocence. There is some psychological validity to this system, since the emotional stress of lying makes speaking smoothly more difficult, but the method is not always accurate. Given how important it was to recite the oath of innocence perfectly, professional compurgators soon appeared for hire to recite a perfect oath. Some authorities believe the legal profession evolved from these early hired compurgators, while others favor the idea that lawyers are modern substitutes for the champions of trials by combat. Our modern adversarial judicial system evolved from the belief that God would intervene in combat, ordeal, or oath taking and determine the guilt or innocence of the accused party. Today we hold adversarial trials before a judge or jury, and the verdict is determined by the argument they believe. Is this the best way to administer justice?

Is the English adversarial system more effective at finding truth than the European inquisitorial system, for example? Studies by John Thibaut and Laurens Walker found that if the facts known to attorneys are accurate, the European inquisitorial system is better at finding truth than the English adversarial system. On the other hand, if the facts known to the attorneys are ambiguous, the English adversarial system is better at uncovering the truth.[16] Because we generally can't be certain whether the facts known to attorneys are accurate, we can't determine which system is superior by empirical research alone, although evidence is often ambiguous at trial, suggesting that the English adversarial system may be more accurate at finding the truth.

Another argument for the adversarial system is the belief that when two opposing attorneys try to prove their client's facts and disprove the opponent's facts, the truth is more likely to prevail. The assumption is that our adversarial system leaves the truth standing when the trial is over, much like trial by combat, ordeal, or compurgation, when God was assumed to intervene and determine the verdict. Before we abandon the English adversarial system, we should consider whether there is another legal system that can uncover the truth more often. Currently we know of no other legal system that does a better job of finding the truth and protecting legal rights than the English adversarial system for most cases. But is the adversarial system a good way to handle divorces?

The adversarial divorce was introduced in family law to limit the number of "frivolous" divorces in the United States. Has the system worked? Collaborative experts feel that the adversarial system imposes too many collateral costs on divorcing couples and their children to be an effective divorce process.[17] They argue that the best interests of parents and their children are rarely served by subjecting the parents to an adversarial divorce, because it often makes the parents hate each other. As a result, they do a poor job of parenting their children after the divorce. Because adversarial divorces cause emotional and financial damage to couples and their children, other dispute resolution methods have been developed to mitigate the harm. Examples of alternate dispute resolution methods for divorcing couples include mediation and collaborative divorce.

Mediation

Mediation was introduced more than a generation ago to encourage clients and their attorneys to resolve disputes through settlement discussions guided by a neutral mediator, who would help them resolve their disagreements through negotiation and compromise.[18] Mediation works because the neutral third-party expert is able to clarify areas of disagreement, offer new settlement options to both parties, help each party see the strengths and weaknesses of their case, and gently nudge them toward a settlement. Currently, nearly 80 percent of litigated cases are settled by negotiation or mediation prior to trial. A more recent legal procedure is the collaborative divorce, a process guided by a trained team of professionals who help a divorcing couple settle their dispute through interest-based negotiation, without going to court.

Collaborative Divorce

A collaborative divorce offers many benefits compared with adversarial litigation, including privacy, lower cost, transparency, client control, and convenience. In addition, it preserves family relationships, protects children, allows creative settlement solutions, and minimizes post-divorce conflicts.[19] Everything said or produced during a collaborative divorce is confidential, so none of the collaborative team can be compelled to testify about what happened during the divorce, and no collaborative documents have to be disclosed if the case ends up in litigation. In a litigated divorce everything is in the public record. Moreover, the average cost of a collaborative divorce is less than the average cost of a litigated divorce. Participants in the collaborative process voluntarily produce all relevant financial and family information, so they avoid the lengthy and expensive discovery fights characteristic of litigated divorces. Moreover, documents and assets are less likely to be hidden during a collaborative divorce, because the parties agree to be transparent. They also develop trust during the process, which helps them work out a settlement that meets the goals and interests of both parties and facilitates co-parenting after divorce.

Collaborative divorces are settled through negotiation, so clients control the outcome and don't turn their future over to a judge or jury. By contrast, the typical litigated divorce is controlled by attorneys—who dictate strategy and determine which documents to produce—and a judge, who makes rulings during hearings that determine the content of a settlement or judicial order. Collaborative meetings are scheduled at the convenience of the parties, which is a real advantage for busy couples who can't easily take time from work to attend lengthy hearings scheduled at the convenience of the court and attorneys. The collaborative process helps divorcing couples communicate, respect each other, and work together to reach a settlement. However, a litigated divorce brings out the worst in people, makes them hate each other, and destroys any hope that they can work together constructively when the divorce is finished.

Children are never put in the middle of a collaborative divorce. If the collaborative team needs information about the children, a child specialist is engaged to interview them and produce a report. In a litigated divorce, children may be forced to meet with a judge in chambers to tell him or her where they want to live or endure a custody evaluation if the parents can't agree on a parenting plan. Litigation is destructive of the parent-child relationship. The collaborative process allows clients and their attorneys to reach creative settlements not available in court, while a judge will usually order standard possession, guideline child support, and an equal split of community assets. The parties can creatively structure a collaborative settlement to meet their unique needs.

Collaborative settlements can produce shared custody, out-of-guideline child support, contractual alimony to take advantage of differing tax rates, and unusual divisions of the community estate; the settlement is negotiated with the unique goals and interests of both parties in mind. Collaborative clients learn to respect each other and recognize that fighting is not productive. Consequently, they are able to co-parent effectively after the divorce, and they rarely go back to court to fight about the terms of their divorce. Many litigated divorces end up back in court to resolve disputes that could have been worked out earlier had the parties been reasonable.

Chapter 2

History of Marriage

All modern societies (except the Na people of China) organize family life around the institution of marriage.[20] The requirements, rituals, and rules associated with arranging and authenticating a marriage have varied throughout history. Marriages are formed for personal, economic, political, social, and religious reasons, as well as for sexual access and reproduction. Some anthropologists argue that sex and reproduction are sufficient to define a marriage, but others believe marriage involves a collection of rights and duties beyond sex and children. Marriage among Roman Catholics was believed to be a visible sign of God's grace.[21] How do anthropologists define marriage?

Definitions of Marriage

Based on common factors found in marriages around the world, matrimony authorizes sexual relations and the production of legitimate children, governs financial transactions within the family, and determines how assets, titles, social status, and power may be inherited. Additional factors include the rights and obligations of husband and wife toward each other and their children, relations with in-laws, sex roles, rights to property and labor, creation and sharing of a marital estate, support of the family, and management of children. Marriage traditionally involves the union of a man and a woman who engage in sexual relations, produce legitimate children, and cooperate economically to support their family. But definitions of marriage have

changed dramatically through the centuries.[22] Some modern legal definitions allow same-sex marriage as well as unions between a man and woman.

Origins of Marriage

Primates, our closest biological relatives, don't organize their sexual lives
and care of offspring around mated pairs; instead, they engage in group
sex.[23] Experts believe human females marry when they are ready to have
children and to gain assets.[24] Human males marry for sexual access and
to increase the likelihood that children are related to the husbands. There
are other ways humans could organize their mating behavior. For example, males might invest in sexual competition with other males and breed
with several females, while human females could have sex with multiple
mates. However, serial monogamy is the common way people mate. Why
has pair bonding and marriage become nearly universal among humans?

Most authorities believe some early human females developed a genetic preference for mating with successful males who could provide them
with assets. These assets allowed women to produce more viable offspring
than females using other mating strategies. This more successful female
mating strategy naturally produced future generations with a genetic tendency to marry. The process produced modern humans who are genetically programmed to marry, have sex, and produce children.[25]

Serial monogamy probably developed because divorcing one mate
and remarrying another increases the genetic variability of each parent's
offspring, enhancing the chance that their children will survive and re-
produce under varying environmental conditions. This means that marrying, divorcing, and remarrying are probably inherited genetic behaviors
among humans.[26] Historically, men acquired wives by capture, purchase,
family arrangement, or mutual consent.

Marriage by Capture

Some early marriages occurred by capture, when a bride was taken by
force during a tribal raid. "Bride-napping" still occurs today in a few countries.[27] Marriage by capture was common among early North and South

American Indian tribes. If the female was high ranking, her tribe might try to recapture the woman, which could trigger a war. Marriage by capture was probably not the dominant way of acquiring mates, even among ancient hunter-gatherer groups; it was likely used mostly when single women were scarce in the tribe. As a quaint historical legacy of marriage by capture, some modern primitive tribes stage sham fights between the families of the bride and groom prior to a marriage.

Marriage by Purchase

Paying money to the bride's family was common in ancient cultures.[28] Ancient Greek men generally received dowries from their bride's fathers when they married.[29] It's believed that ancient Roman men sometimes purchased brides, although that type of marriage was uncommon in ancient Rome. In England, the bride-price was fixed by statute. Ancient Jewish law required a husband to set aside a certain sum of money for his wife in the event she was widowed or divorced. Similar legal requirements exist today in the form of statutes governing property division, alimony, child support, and inheritance. Some modern cultures give lavish gifts to the bride and groom, including household furniture, expensive jewelry, watches, etc. Teutonic tribes required a husband to pay the bride-price to his wife, so she would be supported if he died or they divorced. Another common practice among ancient cultures was for a dowry to be paid by the bride's family, which had to be returned to the wife if she was widowed or divorced.

Marriage by purchase may have evolved from the earlier practice of marriage by capture, when it became common for the groom or his family to pay the bride's family to buy peace. No matter what its origin, marriage by purchase became a common way of contracting marriages as societies accumulated wealth. The giving of wedding gifts may be a residual legacy of marriage by purchase.

Arranged Marriages

Throughout human history marriages have been arranged by families. Usually a bride-price or dowry was negotiated as part of the marriage contract, depending on the wealth and status of the families involved and the bride's desirability. The price for a high-status bride was often a herd of cattle, a hoard of gold, or a substantial tract of land. Aristocratic families married their daughters to powerful men in exchange for social status, political power, or the establishment of economic ties. Today, wealthy American women sometimes marry impoverished European aristocrats in an informal exchange of money for social position and aristocratic title. Ancient cultures allowed the groom to perform a service to the bride's family as a substitute bride-price. This practice was common in Biblical times. For example, Jacob served Laban, his mother's brother, for fourteen years in exchange for the right to marry two of his cousins, Leah and Rachel.[30]

Among ancient Chinese families, the father of the groom was required to pay a negotiated sum to seal the purchase of a bride for his son.[31] According to the Code of Hammurabi, it was customary for a man to pay a bride-price, which was returned if she died without producing children. Under Talmudic law, consent to marry was formalized by the exchange of *haseph* (money), and without the exchange the contractual marriage was invalid. During the Middle Ages, grooms began giving their brides gold, silver, or bronze rings instead of money as a token of love and commitment. The ritual of exchanging engagement and wedding rings survives to this day among many societies around the world.[32]

Mesopotamian Marriages

Arranged marriages were common in ancient Mesopotamia, and auctions were held once a year in villages, where young women were sold to the highest bidder. More often, marriage contracts were negotiated between Mesopotamian families outside the bride auction. There is evidence that some Mesopotamian men and women lived together without a marriage contract, although they were not officially married and lacked certain legal rights common to formally married couples.

There were four stages to a Mesopotamian marriage: the marriage contract, payment of the bride-price, a marriage feast, and the bride moving to her father-in-law's house to consummate the marriage. As has been true in all cultures, a major purpose of Mesopotamian marriage was to produce children. If the wife proved barren, a man was allowed to take a second wife, although he could not divorce his first one. Some historians believe that Mesopotamian marriages were based on love, given the many love poems and songs that have survived. Others believe these romantic poems were written about love separate from marriage.

Marriage in Ancient Greece

Ancient Greek marriages were usually arranged by the families, although professional matchmakers were sometimes hired to find a suitable match for an important male. Every ancient Greek city had its own marriage customs, although the rules were informal, and no specific ceremony was necessary to authenticate an ancient Greek marriage. Greek men generally married in their mid to late twenties and Greek women in their late teens. A bride-price was paid, the couple lived together, and the marriage was deemed valid. Greek women had few rights. In Sparta, marriage was so important that individuals who married late were subject to criminal prosecution. Spartans believed it was the duty of every healthy male to produce children for the state. If a marriage did not produce children, Spartan husbands and wives were allowed to divorce and remarry or live with others to produce children. Ancient Greek men were required to marry before age thirty-five or pay a fine, because they were not producing children.

Except for arranged political marriages, most girls weren't betrothed until they were of childbearing age. Greek men could keep concubines while they were married if their wives consented, and they could legitimize the concubines' children. Greek citizens were obligated to marry other Greeks. Brothers and sisters were allowed to marry if they were not born of the same mother (genetically similar to first cousins). If a Greek father died without male heirs, his oldest daughter was required to marry her nearest male kinsman, and her inheritance belonged to her new husband. Marriages during the winter and under a full moon were thought to be advantageous in ancient Greece.

Marriage in Ancient Rome

Marriage between Roman citizens was supposed to be monogamous, although Roman males could have sex with slaves or consenting single women while they were married. Some ancient civilizations allowed men to take multiple wives, but Romans practiced monogamy.[33] Roman monogamy was adopted by early Christian leaders and remains the norm in most Western societies, although many other nations authorize polygamy. The purpose of Roman marriage was to produce children. A Roman wife's property transferred automatically to her husband when she married. A legal Roman marriage required an agreement by the bride and groom, consent of their fathers, and a ceremony before witnesses. Husbands and fathers had absolute power over wives and children in ancient Rome. Gifts between Roman spouses were considered conditional loans that could be collected on divorce. Like the Greeks, Roman citizens had to pay a tax to remain single, because they were not producing citizens.

A dowry was sometimes paid by a bride's family to the Roman groom, to cover his wedding expenses. While the marriage endured, the dowry belonged to the husband. However, the dowry generally reverted to the wife's family if a divorce was initiated by the husband or if he died. If a couple with young children divorced, the wife could claim a share of the husband's property for her children if she gained custody, although the children usually remained with their father. The marriage contract generally specified how a dowry would be handled on divorce or death of the husband. Many marriage rituals evolved over the years.

Marriage Rituals

No matter what the method of arranging a marriage, certain rituals had to be performed to make it valid, although these varied among cultures.[34] The rituals often included betrothal (a promise to marry) and a wedding (the actual marriage). Among ancient Romans and early Christians, betrothal and the wedding were usually held the same day, but for many other cultures, there was a significant interval between these events.

Marriage Proposals

When the bride and groom had a choice about whom to marry, the most common ritual was for the male to propose and offer his potential bride a token or symbolic article (similar to an engagement ring), and she was allowed to consider his offer. She could accept his offer of marriage or reject it by returning the token or symbolic article. There was certainly pressure exerted by families about the choice of a marriage partner when males and females selected their own mates, but the bride and groom in many ancient and some modern cultures had a choice of mate.

Publicity

A major purpose of ancient marriage rituals was publicity for a legitimate marriage to distinguish it from an illicit sexual union. Publicity was achieved in several ways, including an announcement to the village or the performance of various public ceremonies signaling a betrothal and wedding. Many ancient tribes accepted obvious cohabitation and public acknowledgment of the marriage as sufficient publicity to form a legal marriage.

A common-law marriage can be achieved in Texas by a couple cohabiting and holding themselves out as married. Many societies require witnesses to attend the marriage ceremony in order for it to be valid. Among the modern Bantu, consummation of the marriage has to be witnessed by a group of women before it is legitimate. If the groom is impotent, the marriage is invalid.

Feasting and Dancing

A common method of announcing a marriage has been by a feast. Modern marriages have similar rituals, involving a wedding ceremony and a reception. Another common ritual was the joining of hands by the bride and groom. Some cultures tied the bride and groom's hands together during the wedding ceremony as a symbol of commitment.

Wedding Rings

Modern engagement and wedding rings serve a similar purpose to tying hands, because exchanging rings publicly symbolizes the marriage. There are various superstitions associated with engagement and wedding rings; chief among them is that if a ring is lost the marriage will fail.

Consummation of the Marriage

Most cultures have required consummation of a marriage for it to be valid. In some societies couples had sexual relations prior to marriage. Among other societies, the groom spent time after the wedding, but before consummation of the marriage, with his male friends, in a ritual similar to the modern bachelor party beloved by grooms the world over. There are many explanations for delaying consummation following marriage, ranging from bashfulness to superstition.

Marriage Scheduling

Many cultures prescribe certain seasons as the best time to marry. Often the time is governed by phases of the moon, with a new moon or full moon usually favored.[35] Some experts speculate that these beliefs are related to the bride's menstrual cycle, which is associated with phases of the moon. Other cultures believe certain days of the week are best for marrying. Most societies mix religious rites into the wedding ceremony, often holding the wedding in a church or holy place.

In the past, families sometimes sacrificed animals and marked the bride and groom's foreheads with blood to symbolize a marriage. An almost universal custom now is for the newly married couple to share a meal. Many cultures break eggs during the wedding, to symbolize fertility. Another ritual is to break pottery or glasses during the wedding ceremony or to have the bride and groom sit on an animal skin and share food. Honey and other sweet foods are often eaten during weddings to ensure the couple have a happy marriage. Sometimes drums are beaten, guns fired, and fireworks exploded to scare away evil spirits and protect the couple from harm. In ancient times, arrows were shot into the air to warn away evil spirits. Carrying a bride over the threshold is common among many cultures, including our own. Some societies have required the bride and groom to consent to marry.

Consent to Marry

After Rome adopted Christianity as the state religion, a marriage could not be formed without consent of the bride and groom. During the late Middle Ages in Europe and Colonial America, parental consent was required if young people wanted to marry before the age of twelve for girls and fourteen for boys. At that time it was easy to marry—all you had to do was say "I do"—but it was more difficult to prove you were married.[36] In modern America, parental consent is required to marry before age eighteen, but the marriage is recorded and easy to prove by producing a formal certificate.

Men generally mate with one female at a time and support their wives and children in return for sex and the likelihood that their children are genetically related to them. Marriage allows men to avoid the wear and tear of competing with other males for sexual favors and increases the likelihood that their children will survive. Males prefer to marry young healthy females who are energetic, have conspicuous curves, and are nurturing, while females prefer men who have assets to support them and their children. A recurring issue concerning the institution of marriage is whether individuals should marry one person or several.

Monogamy or Polygamy

Throughout history, most humans married at least once during their lifetimes. As we saw earlier, in the 1960s approximately 85 percent of Americans married at some time during their lives; today only about 50 percent of American adults are married.[37] The majority of humans practice serial monogamy, but many countries allow a man to take more than one wife if he can support them, and the frequency of polygamy increases if there are fewer men.[38] Women prefer not to share their husbands with other wives, because they have to compete for attention and resources, so they avoid polygamy if possible. Bonds among two-wife polygamous marriages are more stable than among three-wife marriages, although we are not certain why.[39] Many men prefer sexual variety and the opportunity to increase their reproductive success by marrying several women if they can afford a harem. Women agree to enter a harem when it's the best way for them to acquire resources for themselves and their offspring, especially if eligible men are scarce. Few men have multiple wives, and it's rare for a woman to marry more than one husband at the same time. Sometimes there is conflict between groups who support monogamy and those who support polygamy.

For example, after the Civil War, traditional American monogamous marriage came under attack from the Church of Jesus Christ of Latter-Day Saints (the Mormon Church) in the Utah Territory, because their practice of polygamy was against United States law. The Mormon Church threatened to pass state laws legalizing polygamy once they were admitted into the Union. Not only did Mormons condone polygamy, but Utah allowed nonresidents to divorce under its liberal laws. Mormons were able to avoid prosecution and punishment for having several wives because Utah didn't register marriages. Utah women favored polygamy because they believed monogamy caused adultery, prostitution, and abortion. During the 1880s, Congress made it unlawful to cohabit with more than one woman and required all persons who wanted to vote in national elections to take an oath that they did not live in a polygamous relationship. In 1890, the Mormon Church issued a proclamation stating that no Mormon should contract a marriage against the laws of the United States. However, plural Mormon marriages continued in secret for years, and they exist even today in some isolated fundamentalist communities in Utah and a few other states.

Marriage in Colonial America

Colonial laws and customs encouraged monogamy, while Native American tribes practiced polygamy because many young men had been killed in war and there was a surplus of women.[40] Under English and colonial law, a married couple formed a single unit, with the husband as head and the wife having few rights except through her husband. This is the reason women usually take their husbands' names when they marry. Christianity reinforced English common law by making the husband head of the family. After the American Revolution, marriage evolved into a social contract that required individual consent. Husbands and wives began to enjoy more equal rights, although even today there are residual gender differences in sex roles and economic opportunities in most Western countries and large gender differences in some Middle Eastern countries, such as Saudi Arabia.

Early American political writers believed that monogamous marriage was the best way to develop public-spirited citizens who would support and defend the Republic against all enemies. After the American Revolution and the drafting of the US Constitution, authority over marriage was retained by the states, while the federal government was given responsibility for the post office, foreign relations, Native American relations, the addition of new states, and the question of freeholder rights versus the rights of slaveholders among the states prior to the Civil War. The balance of power between states and the federal government shifted after the Civil War in favor of national control, except in the area of family laws.

Regulation of Marriage

In America, states enjoy exclusive authority to control marriage and divorce, although these laws must be consistent with the US Constitution. Most states require a marriage license and authorize certain officials and the clergy to conduct weddings. Even though states have different laws, they are required to recognize the laws of other states, so a nominally similar system of marriage and divorce law has gradually developed in America. Today most marriages and divorces are conducted through county courts.

Prior to the Civil War, a number of groups began advocating for "free love" and lobbied to get government out of sexual matters.[41] These groups did not intend for people to be promiscuous. Instead, free love meant that when a married couple no longer loved each other, they should be free to divorce and marry someone else. At that time, no-fault divorce was a scandalous idea, although it's common today. The Civil War significantly affected the institution of marriage in America, because so many men were killed fighting it.

Over six hundred thousand men died in the American Civil War, and this limited marriage opportunities for an entire generation of American women. This was particularly so in the South, where one in five white men were killed during the war.[42] Many young women were widowed or never married, and a significant number of them lived without the protection and dominance of men after 1865. As a result of their experiences as single women, American marriage and divorce laws began to change after the Civil War. Marriages became more equal, and divorce and other legal rights for women were gradually liberalized.

When the Thirteenth Amendment was proposed after the Civil War, stating that "All persons are equal before the law, so no person can hold another as a slave," many legislators pointed out that this principle could be applied to the relations between parent and child, guardian and ward, and even husband and wife. To protect the authority of men and parents, the Thirteenth Amendment was changed to outlaw slavery without making any statement about the equality of persons. When freed male slaves were given the right to vote, women protested that they should have the same right. However, it wasn't until the twentieth century that women gained the right to vote in America.

Chapter 3

Economics of Marriage

The roles of husband and wife have varied substantially over generations and among different cultures but have generally involved support and care of the family and home. Among ancient hunter-gatherer tribes, men and women both performed essential economic tasks, so gender roles were likely more equal than during agricultural or industrial periods.[43] When humans developed farming, domesticated animals, built towns, and accumulated property, women's economic and social roles deteriorated. Darwin proposed a theory of genetic selection to explain these differences, based on sexual characteristics. Some authorities have suggested that these genetic traits cause sex role differences, while others argue that sex role differences are caused exclusively by social factors.

Division of Labor

When hunter-gatherer tribes migrated in search of game, and planting was done with sticks, women and children collected food and tended gardens while men hunted and protected the tribe. This division of labor produced and maintained a rough gender equality within the tribe, because both sexes performed essential economic tasks. When some genius invented the plow, pulled by an ox or horse, the economic roles of males and females changed. The plow is believed to have transformed the economic, social, and political relationships between men and women.[44] Because of differences in upper-body strength, men took over the primary role of food production, while women were relegated to harvesting, preserving, cooking, weaving, sewing, managing the household, and raising children. Wives became economically subordinate to their husbands, because men controlled the means of production in agricultural societies. Labor essential for survival was controlled by men, and they gained economic, social, and political power over their wives and children as a result. Women were no longer viewed as economic equals within the family.

Women's Status

Three factors contributed to the decline of women's economic, social, and political status following the hunger-gatherer period of human history. One was the shift from hunting and gathering to farming and ranching. The second was the stratification of power as societies became more complex and government developed. The final factor was war and the defense of territory. Following the development of agriculture, men owned or worked the land, while women performed subordinate economic roles. With the advent of farming and ranching, populations increased, and it became essential to govern the nation and defend territory. Ruling and warrior classes became an important part of society and populations became more specialized.[45] Because government and war were primarily conducted by men, their economic and political power grew.

Once farming became established and private property accumulated, men wanted to ensure that they passed their land, status, and power to sons who were genetically related to them. To assure the paternity of their sons, husbands demanded sexual fidelity from their wives, so they could believe their offspring were genetically related to them. The pressure to be sexually faithful caused women to lose more economic, social, and political power and has produced a sexual double standard for men and women that makes equality more difficult.[46] As a result, the sexual equality that existed in hunter-gatherer tribes shifted toward male dominance.

Marriage developed to satisfy sexual needs and produce children, so abortion was discouraged, adultery was punished, barren women were divorced or replaced, and husbands wanted sexual fidelity from their wives. However, even when power was vested in men, women were able to exert considerable control over day-to-day household activities, husbands, and their children, based on wealth, class, sexuality, maternity, and marriage.

Women throughout history have been able to control men through social status, economic power, and sexuality. Pretty young women have controlled powerful men for centuries through sexual attraction. Mothers nurtured, trained, and controlled their young sons, and wives were masters over servants and children within the household. Anthropologists distinguish between authority that is usually held by men and power that is often wielded by women.[47] In the past, women were used as bargaining chips in arranged marriages with rich and powerful men, and they often had little choice in these arranged marriages.

Arranged Marriages

For thousands of years, marriages were arranged between families who knew each other and believed the match to be good for both families. Arranged marriages were formed for economic, political, or social reasons, but the families hoped couples would learn to love each other and have a happy marriage.[48] The families were supportive of the young couple in an arranged marriage. Studies show that arranged marriages, in which a couple is expected to fall in love after the marriage, have slightly lower divorce rates compared with consensual marriages, where the couple falls in love first and then marries.[49] Experts believe arranged marriages have lower divorce rates because couples enter the relationship with more realistic expectations, their families are supportive, the spouses know and trust their parents, and they each believe the person they are marrying is serious about making the relationship work.

In a marriage based on romantic love, expectations are high, and when these expectations can't always be met, the parties often decide that divorce is the answer rather than trying to compromise their differences and make the marriage work. The most important arranged marriages were among the ruling classes, and these were negotiated with care.

The Marriage Game

Arranging aristocratic marriages was a serious game historically, played by families who betrothed their sons and daughters to "desirable" off- spring from other powerful families to form alliances and enhance their economic, social, and political positions.[50] New kings or emperors who won a throne often tried to solidify their power by marrying the widow, sister, or daughter of the prior ruler. The goal of ambitious young males was to marry the daughter of an older ruler who had no sons. When the ruler died, the son-in-law hoped to control the kingdom through his wife; this meant he had to be strong and ruthless enough to hold power in the face of the dead king's brothers or cousins. Aristocratic mothers were also ambitious for their sons.

Queens paid special attention to the status of their sons and schemed to advance their eldest son's position as successor to a ruling husband and father. These power contests produced intense rivalries and bitter com- petitions among and within aristocratic families before and after a ruler died or became disabled. To avoid these competitive problems, Egyptian pharaohs married their sisters or first cousins in an attempt to keep loyal- ties aligned within the family.[51] Other rulers in various countries and ages tried marrying several wives to establish alliances with many powerful noble families within the kingdom and strengthen their power. However, this strategy produced competing heirs with powerful families support- ing their claims to the throne, often triggering civil war when the ruling father died. Marriages among the upper classes were arranged to enhance social status, political power, and national alliances, while middle and lower-class marriages were contracted primarily for economic advantage.

Middle- and Lower-Class Marriages

Marriage was important among the middle and lower classes, because husbands and wives worked together tilling the land, managing shops, and raising food for their family. Marriages during the middle ages involved two stages: betrothal, which involved the exchange of property, and the wedding itself.[52] Business partners sealed financial agreements by contracting marriages between their families to ensure the completion of contracts and to guarantee business arrangements. Among the common folk, marriage was based on who would best serve the needs of the landowner, tradesman, craftsman, or small farmer. Lower-class families wanted to marry their children to husbands or wives who were frugal, industrious, healthy, and knowledgeable about managing a farm, running a business, or organizing a household. These marriages were usually economic arrangements rather than love affairs. Small farmers wanted to marry into landed families, craftsmen courted daughters of guild families, and merchants married into trading families to ensure the right business connections. Marriages also determined who inherited family property when the father died and conferred important rights on legitimate male offspring.

Property Rights

For centuries marriage has been the main way property is transferred, social networks established, and political power consolidated. Wealthy and powerful families have competed for the best marriages to enhance their status, financial security, and power. A commoner could not hope to marry a higher-class spouse, because he could neither afford the bride-price nor meet the social, financial, and political criteria required to marry within the aristocracy. A bright, hardworking, and good-looking commoner might be able to marry into a well-off middle-class family and enhance his economic prospects. Beautiful daughters were sometimes offered to wealthy men as second wives or mistresses in return for financial, social, or political advantages for her family.

Only recently have love and individual choice become the norm for selecting a mate. In the last century, Western women have accumulated significant legal and economic rights that allow them to select a mate based on love rather than economic considerations. However, women in many other countries are still economically and socially oppressed.[53] Modern societies have come full circle, so marriage today is similar to mating among ancient hunter-gatherer tribes, where males and females were more nearly equal and individuals could mate with anyone who would have them.

Even in historical times, some women accumulated money and power by being in the right place at the right time and inheriting property from their father or husband when he died without a legitimate son. But in modern India, where women have legal rights to inherit, their parents often gift property to sons rather than allow daughters to inherit.[54]

Female Inheritance

Some marriages don't produce male offspring, either because the couple can't have children or they produce only daughters. For centuries Western society didn't recognize the legitimacy of bastard sons, so legitimate daughters inherited their father's property if he died without a legitimate male offspring. About 20 percent of all marriages produce only daughters, so some women inherited substantial wealth from their fathers when they died. When a father died without a legitimate son, the eldest daughter usually inherited his assets, and she could become quite wealthy. Also, some widows controlled substantial wealth prior to the industrial age and enjoyed considerable power and status when their husbands died, especially if they had no legitimate sons. However, only a small minority of individuals inherit significant wealth. Young men and women often worked as apprentices or domestic servants so they could afford to marry and support a family.

Supporting a Family

During the Middle Ages, if a female left her family to work as a servant in another household, she served under the control of a housekeeper.[55] If she was frugal, a young household servant could accumulate a modest sum and become an attractive mate for someone from her village. Young men were apprenticed to craftsman in a guild and could not marry until their apprenticeship was finished, although they became desirable mates when they joined the guild. Among wealthy European families, where primogeniture was practiced, the firstborn son inherited all the family property, while daughters were married off to establish political, social, and economic alliances and younger sons were sent into the clergy or military to earn a living.[56] Primogeniture was favored by wealthy families to maintain large land holdings within a single family and avoid splitting an estate among more and more individuals over future generations until each member of the family owned only a minor asset. Living patterns for young adults began to change during the middle ages.

During the middle ages couples began establishing separate households apart from their parents. This was different from earlier living arrangements, in which married sons and daughters generally remained in their parents' homes and were subject to the authority of parents and grandparents while the older generations lived. This arrangement still exists among many Chinese families.[57] Among Chinese, Japanese, and Indian societies today, marriage occurs at a fairly young age, and children are produced quickly. This is because the young parents don't need to be economically self-sufficient before marrying and having children, since they are supported by their parents while they raise a family.

Gender and Economics

Gender inequality is generally based on economic and social power. In earlier times, males owned land and other means of production, or they worked to support their family, while women stayed home to manage the household and raise their children. Cohabitation and complementary economic contributions to the household were sufficient for the formation of a family and the legitimization of the children in most cultures. As women became better educated and entered the workforce, the balance of power gradually shifted. Educated working women were no longer dependent on their husbands for support, so they gained a more equal role in marriage and society.[58]

Prior to modern times, most working women dropped out of the labor market to raise their children when they married and became pregnant. In many modern Western countries, women work and have children out of wedlock or marry and pursue both a family and career. However, in many Asian countries, women stay home and raise their children rather than work after they marry.

Indian women, for example, prefer to stay home and raise their children because it's a status symbol in their culture. Now that Indian men are earning higher incomes, their wives are leaving the workforce in growing numbers.[59] The current rate of employment among modern urban Indian women is below 20 percent and falling. Most young Indian women train for a career, begin a job, get married, and then leave the workforce to care for their families. Indian families looking for wives for their sons prefer educated women, but they discourage working outside the home once these women have children. Also, unemployment in India is high, and there is discrimination against married women taking jobs when men are available to do the same work. Optimists point out that many countries have shown similar patterns of falling female employment when large numbers of people shift from agriculture to industry, but the women go back to work after a generation or two. Whether this pattern will be followed in India is unknown, but there is no doubt that marriage contributes to a family's financial success.

Marriage and Financial Success

Marriage is a significant step toward financial stability and economic success for men and women. The vast majority of young adults who earn at least a high school diploma, get a job, marry, and have children are well off economically during their lifetime.[60] On average, married families earn higher incomes than stepfamilies, cohabiting families, divorced families, separated families, and single-parent families. Married women have a higher standard of living than divorced, separated, and never-married women. The only household group with a higher standard of living than married couples are widows, who inherit their husband's assets.

For centuries, marriage was a favored way of cementing alliances between families and gaining social status, economic advantage, and political power. More recently women have rebelled against the perceived constraints of marriage and begun to insist on access to education, careers, and marriage on their own terms. Educated women face a difficult decision after they finish college and enter the workforce or consider marriage. Beginning with Betty Friedan's *The Feminine Mystique*, female authors have struggled to understand what women want out of life.[61] Their options are to stay single and pursue a career, get married and have children, or do both and try to have it all. Most young women fresh out of college are ambitious; they want to pursue a career and generally plan to postpone or avoid marriage and children. What are they doing decades later?

Well-educated young women generally want interesting and successful careers, but things often don't work out the way they expect. The conclusions from various studies of educated working women tell us that they want many different things and their preferences change as they mature. Women channel their ambitious in different ways. Some pursue careers to the exclusion of marriage and family, while others opt out of careers and devote their considerable talents and energies to marriage and full-time parenting. The majority of educated women want to have a career, be married, and raise a family. Feminist authors advise ambitious young women to think carefully about the type of husband they marry, based on their own goals. One of the keys to career success for a high-achieving woman is to find a husband with lower career ambition who will willingly assume the role of stay-at-home-dad, so she can pursue her career full time and not worry about the home and children.[62]

South Korea is a modern example of what happens to marriage and birthrates when women become educated and have career opportunities—they don't want to get married anymore.[63] The fertility rate among South Korean women is one of the lowest in the world and well below the rate of 2.1 children per woman required to keep a nation's population stable. Experts blame this low fertility rate on the preference of young South Korean women for education and a career rather than a traditional marriage. For many of these young women, marriage is not appealing because they feel South Korean men and their families have outdated expectations for wives. Most young South Korean men and their families expect wives to stay home, cook, clean house, take care of children, and devote their time and energy to the success of the children. It's a mother's responsibility in South Korea to ensure that her children do well in school, succeed on the National Exam, and get into a good university. Having children outside of marriage is seen as shameful, and when it happens, babies are often given up for adoption. Modern South Korean women are caught in a bind—do they give up motherhood and have a career, or do they get married, stay home, raise a family, and forego their ambitions? There are no easy answers for these ambitious, well-educated women.

The South Korean government is taking tentative steps to alleviate some of their problems by offering subsidized child care and support for single-parent families. They are attempting to create gender equality in the workplace, but there is a long way to go. The government is also importing traditional brides from neighboring countries for South Korean men to marry. No matter where women live, they earn less pay for similar work. Why is that?

Women's Pay

Modern women's economic status is still not equal to men's, primarily because there are differences in pay for jobs selected mainly by women compared with jobs performed predominately by men.[64] For example, the majority of elementary school teachers are women, and they are paid less on average than are skilled electricians or plumbers, who are predominantly men. Another factor affecting women's pay is the time they take off from work to have and raise children. Maternal leave and "mommy-track" jobs within large corporations tend to segregate women into lower-paying tracts within the same firm and limit these women's chances of career advancement. The choices women make during their careers also have an influence on their income, because they don't accept as much overtime and they make other career choices that tend to lower their pay relative to men in the same field.

Many liberal economists claim that the differences in income between men and women who are doing the same job is based on sexism and must be fixed by government intervention. However, a recent study of workers at the Massachusetts Bay Transportation Authority shows that this claim may not be accurate.[65] The Massachusetts Bay Transportation Authority is a union shop with uniform hourly wages and benefits for men and women who do the same work and follow the same rules. Men and women in the same jobs have the same options about scheduling, vacation, and overtime work. There is little room for giving men preferential treatment under this system. Yet women who worked for the Massachusetts Bay Transportation Authority earned less than men in the same jobs, primarily because men worked approximately 85 percent more overtime hours than women in the same occupations.

Also, men took almost 50 percent less time off for unpaid family leave each year compared with women. Fathers used the extra time to earn more to support their families, while mothers wanted the time off to care for their families. These differences even existed among single-parent households. Single mothers took almost 60 percent less overtime work compared with single fathers. We don't know if these choices were based on personal preferences or economic necessity, but it's clear that differences in the choices females and males make at work account for almost all the differences in wages earned doing the same job. This study supports the commonsense conclusion that men and women have different work and family priorities and that making work rules less flexible probably makes it more difficult for them to balance work and family life in a satisfactory way. Women have more educational and economic opportunities today than ever before, but they still feel oppressed.

Female Independence

When women entered the workforce during and after the Second World War, they became less dependent on their husbands for support. As a result of their work experiences during the war, women demanded a more equal role in marriage, family, and society. Among earlier generations, most working women dropped out of the labor market to raise their children after they married. Today, women marry, start a family, and continue their careers. Alternatively, many single women are having children out of wedlock and raising them on their own. Women are also gaining more legal rights to go along with their economic power. During the twentieth century, women acquired the right to own property, inherit estates free from their husbands' debts, sue in their own names, sign contracts, and draft their own wills. The combination of economic gains from education, a career, and new legal rights allowed women to achieve nearly equal status with men in modern marriage and society.

Chapter 4

Natural Selection, Religion, and Marriage

The most likely explanations of why marriage is nearly universal are the provider theory, male sexual conflict theory, and the inherited tendency of humans to mate, marry, and produce children.[66] The provider theory asserts that marriage evolved because women who had a genetic tendency to mate with men capable of providing food for their children and protection from enemies and predators produced more offspring. Thus natural selection ensured that the tendency to marry passed to future generations.

The sexual conflict theory argues that men naturally compete for sexual access to women and that marriage evolved as an efficient and effective way of keeping order within the tribe by limiting sexual competition among males. This theory assumes that men who married and mated rather than competing for sexual access to women produced more viable children, and natural selection ensured that future generations of human males had an inherited tendency to marry. The provider theory, male sexual conflict theory, and the inherited tendency to marry jointly explain why marriage is nearly universal.

Evolution of Marriage

Women need resources to support themselves and their children, and men are willing to marry, support, and protect their mate and children in return for sexual relations. Men prefer exclusive sexual access to a woman so they can avoid raising other men's children. If there were no organized method of regulating sexual access to women, modern society would probably not survive, because the constant fighting among males for sexual favors would likely destroy any complex civilization. Anthropologists believe that males stayed with the tribe for sex and to defend their wives and children, that some couples had a genetic tendency to form mated pairs, and that those mating patterns produced more viable offspring than other mating systems, causing the institution of marriage to evolve through natural selection.[67]

When hunter-gatherer tribes moved in search of good hunting and foraging grounds, they accumulated few possessions and no permanent dwellings. There were apparently two types of hunter-gatherer tribes—those who had plentiful food and those who had little surplus food available when hunting or foraging failed.[68] These primitive economic systems required that tribal groups cooperate, share resources, and develop a mating system that allowed them to keep peace within a small, close-knit tribal group. Rather than males fighting among themselves over women, anthropologists believe human pair-bonding and marriage evolved to give males access to sex and to supply women and children with food and protection. This theory also assumes that because pair-bonding and marriage produced more children, natural selection ensured that marriage became a universal inherited characteristic among almost all societies.

When our ancestors developed agriculture and ranching, settled in one place, built permanent dwellings, and cleared land for growing crops or raising livestock, inequalities among individuals and groups appeared. When property rights developed in land and livestock, cooperation and sharing diminished within the community. Individuals began to accumulate assets for their own use rather than for the common good, and some individuals or families were more economically successful than others. It's easy to document the early inequalities that developed among agricultural peoples as cities grew, if we look at the varying size of family dwellings. During hunter-gatherer times, a tribe would share a single cave or build temporary shelters of similar size in each new territory where they hunted and foraged. Where humans settled down and built permanent dwellings, we see evidence of economic, social, and sexual inequalities in dwellings of varying size and quality.

Wealthy families formed close-knit social groups and insisted that their children marry within their own class. This had the result of increasing inequalities within society, because wealthy groups enjoyed extra advantages and inherited substantial wealth. With the accumulation of wealth, rich families could demand higher bride-prices for their daughters, and families who could not afford to pay the bride-price were forced to drop out of the competition. If a wealthy husband died and left a rich widow, another male member of his family, usually a brother or uncle, was often obligated to marry her and produce offspring to carry on the family name and inherit the family wealth. Competition among families changed the role of men and women in marriage.

Gender Roles

Division of labor between males and females likely developed early in the evolution of marriage, because women would have to keep their children close for feeding and protection while males went hunting. Until a few thousand years ago, most humans lived in small hunter-gatherer tribes that moved between different hunting and foraging areas, depending on where game or wild crops were most plentiful. They consumed the food they gathered almost immediately.[69] Humans lived in roaming hunter-gatherer bands far longer than they have resided in villages or cities, so human genetic adaptations have probably not caught up to our current environment. Early hunter-gatherer bands generally comprised between two dozen and one hundred individuals, who worked together to forage and hunt for food and offer protection against predatory animals and other hostile tribes.

Experts believe that the key to survival of these bands was cooperation, because no one family could expect to find adequate food every day, and preservation techniques were primitive. By cooperating and sharing food, the tribe was able to take advantage of successful foraging and hunting trips and ensure their survival.[70]

When a male hunting group brought meat home, the individuals who killed the beast would share with other tribal members, and they expected to receive a share of the next kill in return. Mating patterns were important among these early hunter-gatherer tribes because they forged social networks within the group that would ensure food sharing and protection. Sometimes males or females migrated to neighboring groups to marry and form alliances between tribes for peace and mutual protection. These exchanges of spouses between groups also occurred to balance the number of males and females available for marriage within each tribe. Moreover, intertribal marriage produced genetic mixing and avoided inbreeding and its associated defects. Anthropologist and ethnologist Claude Levi-Strauss suggested that men made arrangements for marriages with neighboring tribes and exchanged men and women to establish closer ties between the tribes.[71]

Feminists have argued that men dominate women through arranged marriages.

Arranged Marriage

Marriages negotiated between families were common throughout the world until fairly recently, and they still exist in many cultures. Up until the eighteenth century most marriages were arranged. The customs, expectations, and purposes of arranged marriages varied among different cultures, however. Sometimes the young bride and groom were allowed to meet prior to the marriage and might even have some choice about a mate. More often, the respective families made all the marriage arrangements, and the bride and groom would be introduced only after financial terms had been settled. Even today in India, Pakistan, areas of the Middle East, rural Japan, and some South American countries, arranged marriages are common, although the practice is fading with the advent of more individual freedom and consensual marriage.

A study in India a few years ago found that people who married for love were more in love during the first five years of their marriage compared with couples in arranged marriages, but couples in an arranged marriage were more in love for the next thirty years. Moreover, the divorce rate among couples whose marriages were arranged is lower than among love-based consensual marriages.[72] The traditional rationale for arranged marriages, aside from the economic, social, and political advantages for the family and couple, is that young people are too immature and impulsive to make a good decision about whom to marry. In cultures where arranged marriages are the norm, couples expect to marry and then learn to love each other, while in countries with a tradition of consensual marriage based on romantic love people expect to fall in love, marry, and live happily ever after. Nearly half of marriages in the United States end in divorce, so obviously marrying for love doesn't guarantee a successful marriage.

Arranged marriages reduce differences in religion, caste, socioeconomic background, core values, and education. Arranged marriages also lower the rate of divorce, perhaps because these couples have more realistic expectations about marriage and each other. Marrying for love gives couples a feeling of autonomy and independence. Many individuals believe that love will conquer all and that falling in love with someone before you marry increases the likelihood the relationship will work. Divorce rates suggest that arranged marriages are somewhat more enduring than those based on romantic love, but the way marriages are formed and their success rates depends primarily on the cultural expectations of the individuals and families involved. If they believe that arranging a marriage is the best method, then couples will learn to love each other and generally have a successful marriage. If people believe that falling in love first is necessary for a happy marriage, that's the marital system they will choose. Neither system is inherently better—it depends on people's expectations about how happy marriages are formed.

Consider arranged marriages in Japan.

Japanese Marriage

Arranged marriages among modern Japanese couples, called *omiai*, have a long history and are frequent even today.[73] A majority of modern Japanese couples choose their own marriage partners, but there is still a significant minority who opt for an arranged marriage. A similar phenomenon is happening within other societies, where professional marriage brokers

use questionnaires to match individuals based on shared values and interests. Why do Japanese couples choose arranged marriages? Traditionally
Japanese men were expected to marry by age thirty and Japanese women by
age twenty-five. Japanese women who didn't marry by age twenty-five were
called "Christmas Cake," which means they were unsold by December 25.
There was a significant risk that if a young Japanese woman didn't marry
by age twenty-five, she would never be a bride. Modern Japanese women
marry later and there is less stigma if they stay single, but pressure to wed
early still exists in Japan, and families with older sons or daughters often
turn to marriage brokers to find suitable mates for their older offspring.

Japanese employers prefer to hire married men, because they are considered more reliable and stable. Older Japanese men are turning to omiai
agencies to find a mate if they are unmarried by age thirty, and women
are doing the same if they are unwed by age twenty-five. These agencies
arrange meetings between selected individuals, to see if they get along and
are attracted to each other. If they are attracted to each other, a marriage
can be arranged within a few weeks. Usually they schedule a few dates
before they marry.

After a person signs a contract at the omiai agency, he or she is asked
to complete a profile listing personal preferences and moral values. Often
profiles are completed by the mothers of the prospective bride and groom.
If a match is found based on the submitted profiles, the young couple meets,
usually with a mother or father in attendance. Having parents involved in
contracting the marriage makes sense, because many young Japanese couples live with one set of parents after they marry. Following the first meeting by the young couple, a decision is made whether to continue exploring
this match or look for someone else. Japanese couples usually marry within
a few weeks after their first meeting if all goes well. There is a strong incentive to find a mate quickly, because the omiai agencies are expensive. You
might imagine that the divorce rate among couples who meet by arrangement and marry quickly is high, but in fact arranged marriages have a lower
divorce rate than marriages based on personal choice and romantic love.
Perhaps arranged marriages are not such a crazy mating system after all.

In addition to arranged marriages, many cultures allow wealthy men
to marry more than one wife.

Polygamy

Following the invention of agriculture and the accumulation of assets, some men began to acquire more than one wife, although most men were monogamous because they wanted to ensure that their land was inherited by their own children.[74] While small tribes traveled to find game and forage for food, few men, except perhaps a tribal chief, were able to accumulate sufficient property to support more than one wife. Also, because women's foraging accounted for more than half the calories consumed by hunter-gatherer tribes, they were an important part of the economy, and probably enjoyed essentially equal rights with men. Independent women don't generally tolerate polygamy. Only when these tribes settled down and began farming, ranching, and owning land was it possible for more than a few men to acquire enough wealth and find economically dependent women willing to marry someone who already had one or more wives.

Even though marriage exists among almost all know cultures and societies, there are significant differences in the rules and rituals associated with marriage among religious groups. Three of the most important religious influences on marriage were the Jewish faith, the Catholic Church, and Islam.

Marriage in Ancient Israel

Women in ancient Israel were expected to be virgins when they married, and ancient Jewish men were allowed to take multiple wives. A Jewish man negotiated with the bride's father, offered a gift to seal the betrothal, and paid a price to the bride's father for his daughter. The bride was consulted, but this was apparently a formality.[75] Some experts speculate that the gift was really a sale of the girl to her husband, but Jewish wives were not treated as slaves. Men were the masters of their homes, and Jewish wives could be put to death for adultery, but they were generally respected as companions and mothers. Jewish families preferred marriage between cousins, and Jews were discouraged from marrying outside their religion. Incest was forbidden, but uncle-niece marriages were allowed, and widows were encouraged to marry their dead husband's brothers. Ancient Israeli marriages had three stages: the marriage contract, sexual consummation after payment of the bride-price, and a wedding feast. Once the families signed the marriage contract, the couple was considered formally married, but they could not actually have sex until the groom paid the bride-price.

Besides the Jewish faith, the Catholic Church had a strong influence on Western marriage.

Roman Catholic Marriage

In the fourth century, Emperor Constantine adopted Catholic doctrine as the state religion of Rome, became the protector of the Catholic Church, and derived his divine authority to rule from the pope. Roman emperors and the Catholic Church began restricting the grounds for divorce, although only in the Middle Ages were Catholic marriages declared indissoluble. Catholic marriages were terminated or modified by annulment, separation, or desertion, however.[76] Earlier, ancient Romans had been permitted to divorce their wives if they had abortions, committed adultery, or went to the theater with another man, but easy divorce was curtailed under Catholicism.

When divorced persons wanted to remarry, the clergy could decide whether they were eligible for remarriage within the church. During the early development of Christian doctrine, ancient Roman customs about marriage and divorce were generally followed.

From the eleventh century, celibacy was incorporated into the Catholic priesthood.[77] Early Catholic doctrine held that celibacy and virginity were ideal states for all believers, while marriage, reproduction, and sexuality were inseparable. Marriage was viewed as the only acceptable way to express sexuality and then only with the intent of conceiving children. Sex was not allowed for pleasure among Catholics. After the Council of Trent, a Catholic marriage could not be dissolved, and if divorced individuals remarried, they were believed to be committing adultery.

If a married Roman Catholic had sex with a woman not his wife, his penance under Catholic doctrine was generally one year on bread and water and sexual abstinence for eighteen months. Popes often prescribed excommunication for any man who divorced his wife and remarried. For several centuries after Rome adopted Christianity as its state religion, marriage and divorce were allowed by mutual consent, following earlier Roman traditions. If the divorce was not by mutual consent, the parties were required to forfeit property to their ex-spouse, the state, or the church in order to obtain a divorce. If a husband abandoned his wife, she was required to wait ten years before she could divorce him.

Marriages could be annulled under ancient Roman law if they were contracted under a mistaken belief or without capacity to consent.[78] For example, if the wife turned out to be a slave rather than a free woman, the marriage could be annulled, and the innocent party was entitled to custody of their children. If a wife married again, the husband was entitled to custody of the children, even if he was the guilty party in the annulled marriage. Roman women who wanted to divorce without cause were encouraged to enter a convent, and their property would be divided between the Church and her children. These divorce laws enriched the church and brought many new members into convents, but they created so much discord among Roman citizens that they were later repealed, and divorce by mutual consent was reinstated for Catholic citizens.

What was a married couple to do if they wanted a divorce but one spouse became insane and was unable to consent? They could apply to the emperor, who would grant the divorce on grounds that the marriage had ceased to exist because of one spouse's insanity. The reasoning was that if insanity had occurred prior to marriage, the union would have been void because there was no consent. Thus, if insanity happened after marriage, the same rule should apply, and the marriage didn't exist.

Marriage in the Middle Ages

As the Catholic Church asserted increasing power over emperors and kings, canon law slowly became the norm in Europe, and the available grounds for divorce were restricted. Roman marriages became indissoluble throughout much of Western Europe after the Council of Trent.[79] The Eastern Orthodox Church continued to allow divorce on criminal grounds, but in the West, the availability of divorce was restricted and then outlawed. Powerful popes consolidated their authority over emperors and kings, and canon law gradually replaced secular law for all Christians.

Pope Gregory IX, founder of the Inquisition, promulgated canon law as the supreme legal authority for Europe. The Inquisition was inflicted on the Holy Roman Empire by Frederick II in the thirteenth century. It forced all Christians within his domain to abide by canon law or face excommunication—and often more drastic punishment, such as burning at the stake. Canon law eventually held that Christian marriage was indissoluble because it was a sacrament (a sign of grace). Once a Catholic couple married, the matrimonial bond could not be undone by divorce, according to canon law. The Church claimed exclusive jurisdiction over marriage and prescribed annulment, legal separation, and death as the only ways to end a marriage.

The Protestant Reformation, begun in 1517 by Martin Luther, slowly changed the availability of divorce for Protestants.[80] Luther actually burned a copy of canon law at Wittenberg before a group of citizens. Within a few years, North Germany, Switzerland, Holland, and England repudiated canon law. Luther argued that marriage was a secular contract and could be dissolved on grounds of adultery or malicious desertion. For centuries divorce laws were different depending on whether the state religion was Catholic or Protestant. Protestant Reformers believed that commission of a crime was reasonable grounds for granting a divorce, for example. The Catholic Church believed that canon law was necessary for salvation and therefore could not be avoided by any Christian, even if he or she was Protestant. Many secular jurists adopted the Reformer's views of marriage and divorce.

The other major religious influence on marriage and divorce derives from Islam.

Muslim Marriage

Under Islamic law, marriage is a social contract between a man and a woman who have reached adulthood. The Koran gives men and women the right to choose their mate and states that a man cannot hold a woman against her will. Islamic law promotes the idea that a marriage should be equal, dignified, and reasonable—but conflict may occur when the parents and children don't agree.[81] Islamic men are urged to be monogamous but have the right to marry more than one wife if they are wealthy. A valid Islamic marriage requires a written contract and a civil ceremony before a local authority. Common sources of conflict between Muslim couples include different expectations about the role of a wife in the family, relations with in-laws, adultery, polygamy, and domestic violence. Islamic law favors married couples staying together if possible, and there is strong pressure from families and the community to avoid divorce.

Modern marriages are more liberal than traditional religious marriages and result in divorce more often.

Modern Marriage Patterns

In many Western nations there is acceptance of premarital sex, cohabitation without marriage, egalitarian marriage, having children out of wedlock, easy divorce, and serial monogamy. Moreover, there is no longer any legal distinction between legitimate children born to a married couple and children born out of wedlock. It's not clear what effect this more fluid marriage market will have on women's and children's health, happiness, and long-term survival. When tribes of hunter-gatherer humans formed sexual relationships and the bond broke, the women and children were generally able to feed themselves through foraging. They were cared for by their families and protected by the tribe if they became sick, injured, or disabled. Today, single mothers and their children look to the state for support, and these single-parent families generally end up near the bottom of the socioeconomic ladder.

Within the capitalist system of most Western European counties, the sharing and cooperation characteristic of hunter-gatherer tribes have been replaced with regulated capitalism and a social welfare system established, administered, and supported by the state. It's not clear whether our modern system works better than the earlier hunter-gatherer cooperative system of extended family and tribal responsibility. Moreover, some politicians support the idea that we should reinstate the hunter-gatherer cooperative welfare system on a national scale through socialism.

Chapter 5

Feminism

Keeping a marriage together was traditionally the responsibility of women, but today both men and women are expected to help make a marriage work. John Gottman, world famous American marriage expert, found that couples who like each other, can resolve disputes, make amends after a fight, and treat each other with respect have marriages that last. Conversely, couples who are hostile and detached tend to divorce.[82]

Divorce rates are high all over the world, and no one is certain why, but one factor seems to be women's changing expectations about marriage, family, and their role in society.

Female Expectations

Modern women are demanding more from their marriages, and when their relationships fail to meet their expectations, they often file for divorce.[83] Over 70 percent of all divorces are filed by women, and college-educated women file nearly 90 percent of divorces in their families. A major cause is likely a shift in women's expectations initiated by the feminist movement of the 1960s. Feminists gave us new ways to think about human rights and changed our ideas about sex roles and gender equality.[84] There are at least four types of feminism: Social, Cultural, Global, and Radical.

Social Feminism. Social feminism was first used to describe the women's suffrage movement beginning in the late nineteenth century. The label was later adopted by activists concerned with the special problems of women and children. Early social feminists lobbied to obtain better working conditions for women and children. They advised women against adopting male traits that could dilute their "feminine" characteristics simply to gain political or economic power. Once women obtained the right to vote, they began lobbying for legislation to protect women and children and grant them special government benefits. Social feminists believe mothering should be the primary model for politics because of the unique characteristics of females.

Cultural Feminism. Cultural feminists also believe that cooperation, caring, and nonviolence are needed to resolve social or political disputes. Cultural feminists resist the devaluation of female traits such as nurturance. They argue that females should have their own organizations, run exclusively by and for women. Cultural feminists focus on the emotional and intuitive side of knowledge as opposed to a scientific view of understanding. They are concerned with female nature and reject any scientific theory that denigrates women, including the idea that there are genetic differences between the sexes. Cultural feminists believe that women are oppressed by a patriarchal system and argue that we need to root out and change masculine ideas and institutions that oppress women if we are to have a truly equal society.

Global Feminism. Global feminism is concerned with advancing women's rights internationally. Global feminists point to the patriarchal societies of medieval Spain, the oppressive societies of Islam, and the double standards of modern sexuality as historical and cultural examples of mechanisms that oppressed women. They support the right to motherhood for all women and work for laws to protect migrant women and children from exploitation, whether in the workplace or at home. Global feminists also champion the rights of women to reproductive freedom and total control of their own bodies.

Radical Feminism. Radical feminists call for the restructuring of society to eliminate male dominance in all areas of life. They strive to liberate women from an oppressive, male-dominated society by challenging social norms, opposing sexual objectification of women, and working to raise awareness of rape and physical abuse of women. Radical feminists challenge the very idea of male and female; they argue that we should abolish the notion of gender differences. In an ideal radical feminist world, sexual differences would not matter, and all individuals would be treated equally. Radical feminists believe that women are oppressed by a patriarchal system based on an arbitrary division of society into males and females, in which half the human race bears the burden of reproduction. They assert that men benefit from the oppression of women and exploit women for sex and power.

Radical feminism grew out of the civil rights movement and borrows ideas and methods from the struggle for racial equality in the fight for gender equality. They believe male-dominated institutions contribute to women's subjugation. Radical feminists view marriage, family, and heterosexual roles as masculine means of oppressing women. Few radical feminists advocate the abolition of marriage, but most believe that women should have complete sexual and economic freedom and the opportunity to pursue careers. They expect husbands to help with housework and rearing of children. Feminists believe that many women can't abandon marriage because they rely on their husbands for financial support. Liberated women argue that the institution of marriage should be made less oppressive by instituting significant changes in the roles of husband and wife. Feminism developed after women became better educated and entered the workforce in large numbers after World War II.

Postwar Marriage and Divorce

Immediately after WWII the divorce rate in America soared, as marriages contracted during the war failed and couples who had been separated for years decided to divorce. The majority of returning veterans went to college on the GI Bill, got jobs in the booming economy, married, and moved to the suburbs. At that time, many women stayed home to manage the home and children while their husbands worked. For a decade it looked as if the divorce rate had peaked after the war and was poised to fall. However, three important events intervened during the 1960s that reversed this optimistic outlook: effective birth control, feminism, and the sexual revolution.[85]

Availability of the pill removed the risk of unwanted pregnancy, and premarital sex became an accepted practice among an entire generation. Women demanded more sexual and economic freedom, the institution of marriage came under attack from feminists, women became sexually active prior to marriage, and many educated women pursued careers rather than getting married and raising families. Women's attitudes toward marriage and family changed after the feminist movement redefined sex roles.

Liberated Women

A little-known event occurred in March 1970, when approximately one hundred feminists entered the New York offices of the *Ladies Home Journal* and demanded that the magazine publish an issue dedicated to "liberated" women.[86] After their demand was rejected, about two dozen women staged a sit-in at the *Journal* office until the editor agreed to publish a magazine supplement on "Women's Liberation." The *Ladies Home Journal* was read by over seven million women monthly. Its content was considered demeaning by many liberated women, who believed that its editorial staff presented only a traditional view of American women. Feminists wanted to change the attitudes of women toward marriage and men, and they choose the *Journal* as their initial target. The special feminist issue of the *Ladies Home Journal* included a bill of rights for women and articles arguing that marriage needed major changes, to counteract the oppressive expectations on women by male-dominated society.

Women's Bill of Rights

The National Organization for Women published a Bill of Rights for Women in 1968 that included the following demands: (1) Congress should pass and the States ratify the Equal Rights Amendment to the US Constitution forbidding the abridgment of equal rights on the basis of sex; (2) equal employment opportunities should be available for all women and men, guaranteed by prohibiting sex discrimination in employment; (3) women should have the right to return to their careers after maternal leave protected by law; (4) Congress should revise tax laws to allow deductions for home and child-care expenses for working parents; (5) there should be free child-care facilities funded by the US Government to meet the needs of working parents; (6) women should have the right to education through government fellowships and federal or state training programs; (7) poor women should have the right to job training, housing, and family allowances on equal terms with men and the right to stay home to raise their children; and (8) women should have the right to control their reproductive lives.

Conservative commentators worried about a complete breakdown of marriage and family life if the changes advocated by feminists were instituted. These experts proposed instead that women renew their efforts to make marriages work rather than spend time trying to transform the institution and change their husbands. Feminists experimented with alternate living arrangements and publicized their ideas for others to consider. Liberated women argued that men should share housework and child-rearing and that women should be free to have a career outside the home to counter male-dominated social norms learned during childhood.[87] They also believed that modern women should not simply endure a boring marriage but should search for happiness and fulfillment in a career.

Betty Friedan

In 1963 Betty Friedan, sexual activist and author of *The Feminine Mystique*, published an indictment of postwar American culture and its concepts of marriage, motherhood, and housekeeping.[88] Friedan's goal was to free married women from household routines and encourage them to stop conforming to the ideal of a perfect housewife. Freidan wanted women to enjoy creative work rather than being shackled to a household routine. She argued that American women needed to break free from the rut of raising children and keeping house in order to be psychologically "complete." Friedan also argued that women didn't need husbands to make them "whole." However, she recognized that most women wanted to marry and have children, so she encouraged women to expand their horizons and find satisfaction in their careers and marriages. Friedan told women they didn't need to choose between marriage and career—they could "have it all."

She wrote that if husbands objected, they were being childish and should be ignored. Friedan believed that men must accept the idea of liberated women or suffer the consequence of a divorce. She was fine with either outcome, because Friedan believed working women could support themselves and their children without husbands. However, she ignored the social, economic, and personal difficulties many divorced women faced, and she didn't address the developmental problems of children raised in a single-parent home.

Feminists were focused on the oppression of women by society. They believed marriage was structured to oppress wives and that women should become educated, have careers, and marry on their own terms to gain freedom.

Germaine Greer told women that doctors, psychiatrists, priests, marriage counselors, and other authorities were oppressing them with well-meaning but misguided advice about how to fix their marriages; they should ignore their advice because these "experts" were part of a patriarchal culture.[89] Some radical feminists referred to marriage as "slavery" because women were not compensated directly for raising children and caring for a home. Feminists also noted that women were not free, because they had to follow their husbands when they moved to new jobs. Feminists argued that women should have complete control over their bodies, and they believed that romantic love was just another way society oppressed women. In spite of radical feminist ideas, the majority of American women still insisted on getting married before having children.

Jessie Bernard concluded that men and women lived in different marriages. She reported that husbands and wives responded differently to queries about their marriages, showing that they had different attitudes about their relationships. After retirement, Bernard became a leading writer on feminism.[90] She maintained that marriage was hard work, that women were carrying too much of the load, and that it was time for husbands to do more. Bernard also argued that marriage was good for men, because they lived longer and had better mental health compared with single men.

Research does show that married couples are healthier, wealthier, and happier than single or divorced individuals. Bernard also reported that women were more dissatisfied with relationships than men, and married women reported more mental health problems compared with men or single women.

The Total Woman

To counter feminist criticisms of marriage, Marabel Morgan published a book entitled *The Total Woman,* advising wives to stop trying to change their husbands. She advised women to spend more time being the wives their husbands want, letting them know they admire them.[91] Morgan based her advice on the Christian belief that God ordained men to head their families and be respected by their wives. She knew feminists would say she was condoning slavery by making a wife subject to her husband, but Morgan claimed that argument was nonsense. She said that a wife would be accepting the role through her own free will rather than being forced to comply. Morgan also noted that her method of managing a marriage reaped immediate rewards in better marital relationships.

Patricia O'Brien wanted to find out why some couples stayed together while others divorced. She discovered that few marriages are alike and that couples stayed together through good times and bad because they wanted to be married to each other.[92] O'Brien found that married couples who stayed together cherished their common histories. Experts have debated for decades about who should be primarily responsible for keeping a marriage together but have not found an answer acceptable to everyone.

Feminists argue that it's the job of both partners to make a marriage work, while Morgan and other more traditional thinkers proposed that women should take the lead in making a marital relationship succeed. Marriage experts and most Americans believe marriage is important for society, although there is no consensus about how to lower the divorce rate and make marriage work better for parents and children. Most experts agree that marital counseling should be tried before a couple files for divorce, however.

Marriage Counseling

Early in the twentieth century, marriage experts feared that the high divorce rate was destroying American families, and they wanted to foster more stable marriages. Because of the rising divorce rate, many authorities feared the institution of marriage was in crisis, and they wanted to develop tools to fix broken marriages. These experts proposed that counselors be trained to help couples establish more fulfilling relationships through enhanced communication and an empathetic approach to marriage, treating families rather than individuals.[93] In the 1950s, most marriage counselors urged couples to avoid divorce because it was harmful to the children.

Marriage counselors tried to counteract the romantic notion that being married was easy and that couples would live happily ever after once they fell in love. Counselors advised that maintaining a happy marriage required a strong commitment, patience, forgiveness, and hard work. Early marriage counselors noted that most women stayed home and were economically dependent on their husbands. Thus, they believed, women needed marriage more than men and should assume the primary responsibility for managing and maintaining the relationship. Even though feminists argued for an equal division of marital duties, many traditional women accepted the idea that it was their responsibility to maintain the marriage, especially if they were housewives and mothers.

During the 1980s, marriage counseling grew exponentially as more couples tried to save their failing marriages. The American divorce rate declined slightly as couples worked to fix their relationships. However, while divorce rates were stabilizing, more young couples were cohabiting without marrying, and out-of-wedlock births were climbing, putting new stresses on the institution of marriage.[94] The basic concept of what constituted a family was also changing. The traditional idea of a family—with husband, wife, and children living together, the husband working, and the wife caring for the children—was transforming into various domestic arrangements, including gay couples with and without children, divorced mothers raising children, single women having children out of wedlock, and even experiments with communes. As women became more interested in careers, they changed their attitudes toward marriage and the family.

Women's Careers

Women have been working outside the home for centuries, but modern women want lifelong careers rather than jobs for a few years before they marry and start families. Many marriage experts feared that if women committed themselves to a career they would never marry or have families. A study published by researchers at Harvard and Yale Universities suggested that's what was happening among educated females.[95] They found that educated women who had not married by age thirty had only a 5 percent chance of ever marrying. The consensus was that women who committed to careers and postponed marriage would end up single and might not be happy with the result.

The problem for ambitious women was how to balance these competing demands and develop a happy marriage, a successful career, and healthy children. Most experts concluded that dual-career couples needed to understand that marriage, children, and careers took time, and balancing these conflicting goals was difficult. Could husbands and wives handle these competing demands successfully and have a happy marriage? What happened if the wife earned more than her husband? Could that lead to divorce?

Dual-Income Couples

Gary Becker, author and economist, warned that when a wife earned a higher income than her husband, the couple was more likely to divorce.[96] Since most women earn less than men, it's a problem for only about 20 percent of couples. Dual-career marriages in which wives earn more than their husbands often transform sex roles; this can cause confusion and anger between spouses, who no longer know what to expect from each other. Also, some career women view their income as separate from the family income and available for their own use, while they believe their husband's income should be shared and used to support the family. Financial issues have disrupted marriages in the past, but now, with more women working and raising children, financial issues have become a central problem in many marriages. The main disputes involve who should control spending and how much the family should save. When one spouse wants to borrow and spend while the other needs to save, that's a recipe for divorce.

A related issue among dual-career couples is who should be responsible for doing the housework and caring for the children. In spite of the egalitarian ideal that feminists espouse, surveys show that wives still perform more housework and child-rearing than men. Women's magazines note that wives need to be superwomen to have successful careers, families, and marriages. Advice abounds about how to encourage men to do more housework, including letting them know their wives are feeling overworked and stressed because they are too busy. Moreover, among the demands of work, children, cleaning, and cooking, how will women find the time and energy to enjoy sex? Are they looking elsewhere for sexual excitement? Recent studies suggest that women are straying from the nest more often today. Are women better off with careers and children but no husband?

Women's advocates want more government subsidies for single women with children, but economists suggest that a better approach is to stay married, because women are financially better off with a husband than when divorced or single with children. Many women suffer a significant decline in their standard of living following divorce, while men often enjoy a modest gain in their average standard of living after divorce. By contrast, married couples enjoy a significant financial advantage so long as they don't divorce.[97] Tales abound of divorced women who went from luxurious lifestyles to relative poverty.

Conflict and divorce are also harmful of children.

Divorce and Children

High-conflict divorce creates serious problems for children. A longitudinal study by Judith Wallerstein showed that divorce was harmful to children's development even twenty-five years later.[98] In spite of the findings that divorce is economically damaging to women and psychologically damaging to children, many American women file for divorce every year. What's the answer to these problems? Conservative commentators argue that we should return to more traditional values, with clearly defined gender roles, to lower the divorce rate. These experts believe marriage is not a consensual contract that can be broken at will but a covenant with God and a permanent union that should not be dissolved. They believe married women should devote themselves to their children and families rather than careers. Religious leaders also believe wives should submit to the leadership of their husbands to make marriage work.

Some authorities have suggested abolishing no-fault divorce, but there is little legislative support for that idea. We certainly need to address the problem of divorce, but going back to indissoluble marriages or a fault-based divorce system that encourages perjury is probably not the answer. Also, studies show that children from severely dysfunctional homes are better off when their parents separate and stop fighting, so all divorces are not bad for children.

Liberal commentators argue that men are not taking enough responsibility in marriage and need to be more accommodating. Younger men are working harder on their relationships. They read advice books, attend marital counseling, do more housework and child care, and are generally more committed to working on their relationships than their fathers were. The divorce rate among this demographic group is lower than among older generations, partly because they are cohabiting more frequently rather than getting married. However, younger women still spend more time doing housework, and they are primarily responsible for raising the children. A successful marriage requires commitment from both husband and wife, and if one spouse is seriously considering getting a divorce, for whatever reason, the marriage is probably doomed.

Chapter 6

Modern Marriage

For generations most marriages were arranged for economic advantage, political power, social connections, and useful in-laws. However, during the eighteenth century some individuals began selecting their own mates based on romantic love. The idea that a marriage should be based on romantic love was attractive to liberals; it promised freedom and personal fulfillment. In contrast, marrying for love was viewed by traditional authorities as irresponsible and dangerous, because young people were believed to be too immature to make a good marital choice. In fact, too much love was thought to be a serious problem in a marriage, because it was deemed a form of insanity.[99]

Peter the Great modernized Russian law by outlawing forced marriages and authorizing marriage based on love and personal preference. A marriage contract or engagement proposal was no longer enforceable in court, so couples could change their minds and break off engagements without legal penalties.[100] Marriages based on love were believed to discourage family violence, although physical abuse still occurred. But would love-based marriages last?

Marrying for Love

For generations husbands had been heads of their households, exercising significant control over wives and children. With the introduction of democratic ideas into politics and social life and the shift to marriages based on love, husbands began to lose their authority, and marriages became more egalitarian. Building on the idea of government by social contract, marriage was seen as a democratic agreement between equals. Women began to exert more control over their own lives, but defenders of traditional arranged marriages warned that a relationship based on love and mutual consent would produce high divorce rates and social chaos, because these relationships would be unstable when people fell out of love. The critics were generally correct, but it took generations for the divorce rate to reach its current high level.

Traditional authorities wondered what would hold a romantic marriage together if the couple fell out of love. These experts also worried whether a husband would support his family if he lost control of wife and children. However, divorce rates didn't soar immediately, so people stopped worrying. Liberated women began demanding equal rights and rebelled against the difficulties of getting a divorce, and eventually no-fault divorce laws were introduced in American near the end of the twentieth century. Critics warned that the change would produce a rash of divorces and should be banned if the couple had children.[101] Educated working women began searching for alternatives to marriage and family. They grew more assertive, became interested in careers outside the home, and experimented with premarital sex following the introduction of effective birth control. In spite of these radical changes in attitudes toward marriage, there are still traditional communities within the United States that experience almost no divorce. How do they accomplish that feat?

Marriage in Traditional Communities

Members of the Mennonite and Amish faiths live apart from other American communities and avoid modern conveniences such as automobiles, electricity, and television. They also adhere to traditional ideas about marriage and divorce. Their attitude is "What God joined together, let no one put asunder." Mennonite and Amish marriages succeed through faith and hard work. Because these couples enter marriage with shared expectations about what their roles will be, they have fewer disagreements and maintain their relationships more easily as a result. Also, there is no formal escape valve from marriage within these traditional communities, only informal separation when one party to the marriage leaves the community altogether.

Moreover, Mennonite and Amish women believe that being a good wife and mother is the most important job in the world. They care for babies and are responsible for their children's early education. Traditional marriages seem to work for the Amish and Mennonite communities, and they have very low divorces rates compared with other modern communities.

How did modern marriage norms evolve, and are they the best way to contract marriages?

War and Marriage. During World War II, women did men's jobs and earned good pay. They were reluctant to become dependent again after the war. The GI Bill allowed unprecedented numbers of men to attend college and advance their careers.[102] Married men were offered extra pay and bonuses to help them support their families, and the government made low-down-payment inexpensive mortgages available to veterans so they could buy homes. The US income tax system was changed so that a married man whose wife was not working would pay less tax than a single man earning the same salary. All these changes encouraged marriage. But after the war, over a third of marriages undertaken during the war ended in divorce, because of adultery, quick marriages before men left for war, and the general turmoil caused by depression and war.[103]

In spite of hand-wringing over this high divorce rate, the institution of marriage appeared stable; most newly divorced individuals remarried within a few years and the divorce rate started to drop. The 1950s were considered a golden age for marriage, with nearly 90 percent of Americans marrying. Getting married became a rite of passage for the postwar generation. Young married couples had children at a rapid rate, creating a baby boom, due primarily to better economic conditions and the higher marriage rate after the war. Then the sexual revolution radically transformed marriage and society.

The Sexual Revolution

Freud popularized the power of sex over human behavior and argued that sexual repression was a major cause of many neurotic human behaviors.[104]

Experts acknowledged that women have sexual drives, and popular culture became filled with sexual images. The advertising industry and motion picture producers recognized the appeal of sex and went so far with explicit sexual imagery that governments began censoring motion pictures in 1940. These radical changes in sexual attitudes influenced the dating and mating patterns of American youth. Dating restrictions began to erode after WWII as young men and women gained more freedom. The change in dating patterns was so profound that police departments in many large cities became concerned that these couples were actually engaging in subtle forms of prostitution, exchanging gifts and meals for sex. Experts estimated that approximately 50 percent of young women had sex prior to marriage in the 1920s, and that percentage almost certainly increased in the 1960s. Alcohol and drug use became popular among many young couples as well. Authorities worried that premarital sex, drinking, and drugs would destroy marriage and the family.

During the 1920s and after WWII, women began going to college and taking jobs to support themselves rather than marrying, having children, and becoming dependent on husbands. For many of these young women, marriage became secondary to careers and sexual freedom. When these emancipated women married, they expected more from their husbands than just financial support. If their marriage was not a source of happiness, divorce was just around the corner. Sexual freedom brought problems, however. Over 25 percent of married men and women admitted to having an affair in the 1920s, increasing the number of divorces. The divorce rate doubled from 1880 to 1930, although it still was low by modern standards. Marriage rates began dropping in the 1980s and are lower compared with the prior generation.[105] Our grandparents divorced because of adultery, desertion, impotence, or abuse, but during the 1920s couples began filing for divorce because they were no longer in love.

Conservatives lobbied for stricter, fault-based divorce laws, but that didn't happen, because quick and easy divorces were available in states such as Nevada, Utah, or Florida, across the border in Mexico, or overseas in France. Pressure for easier divorce laws decreased during the 1930s; fewer women were working outside the home because of legislation passed during the Great Depression to distribute available jobs to married men. Also, fewer women went to college and started a career in the 1930s. Experts worried that mating based on consent and love was destroying the stability of marriage, because men and women were becoming self-centered rather than being concerned about their children and the community. Supporters of love-based marriage argued that personal choice created stable marriages.[106]

The reality is that marriages based on love are breaking down at an alarming rate and divorce rates are high.

Liberal reformers advocated basing marriages on love, respect, and total equality because they believed this type of relationship offered the best chance of strengthening the marital bond and family. These liberal experts argued that going back to an authoritarian model of arranged marriages would make women miserable and destroy families. Women were advised that the best way to keep their marriage stable was to be sexually alluring to their husbands.

Modern Marriage

During the 1950s, the idea that everyone should marry and have a family became conventional wisdom. The typical marriage during that decade had a male breadwinner and a female who stayed home, raised the children, and cared for the household. Men and women who stayed single were called "narcissistic" and considered socially and psychologically deviant. Experts believed that women who didn't find fulfillment in homemaking and motherhood were neurotic and needed psychological counseling. This idealization of traditional marriage and family was supported by economic prosperity following the Great Depression and World War II.

Modern marriages were expected to provide sexual fulfillment, emotional happiness, and personal companionship. Even though divorce rates were higher in the 1950s than the 1920s, most experts were not concerned about the stability and viability of marriage. Everyone was optimistic about the future, and few worried about the rising rate of marital dissolutions. Divorce was viewed as a healthy correction for poor marriage choices, and many of the divorced individuals remarried within a few years. Marriage counselors advised couples about how to become better adjusted within their marriage and avoid a divorce. The majority of women still married, stayed home, took care of a house and children, and were dependent on their husbands for financial support—although some women were unhappy with their marital situations.

It's surprising how optimistic experts were about the institution of marriage during the 1950s given the high divorce rate and female dissatisfaction with marriage.

Marriage expectations changed rapidly in the 1960s, and many couples were uncertain about their roles as husbands and wives. Marital experts didn't understand that divorce rates were falling during the 1950s and 60s because of favorable economic, political, and personal factors rather than because modern love-based marriages were inherently stable.

Women's Status

The legal and economic status of women improved after World War II, but husbands were still expected to exercise primary authority within the family and women were still responsible for the home and family. Married women couldn't get credit cards or borrow money in their own names, and they were expected to move when their husbands got new jobs. Moreover, it was legal to pay women less for doing the same work as men. Men were encouraged to get involved in child-rearing, but only on Sunday or holidays. Women were advised to listen to their husbands and never criticize them. Single women who became pregnant were pressured to offer their children for adoption rather than become single mothers—because their babies would have "Illegitimate" stamped on their birth certificates and have limited legal rights as adults.[107]

To better understand how marriages worked, experts began to follow families for several generations. The Institute of Human Development at the University of California, Berkeley began a longitudinal study of families in the 1930s and followed these families through three generations.[108] They found that gender roles became more equal and more married couples said they were happy in their marriages during the 1950s compared with the prior generation, perhaps because of better economic conditions and the end of a major world war. Couples who had endured the Great

Depression and Second World War were delighted with the improved economic and social conditions that ensued. They had lower expectations about life and marriage, which sometimes masked unhappiness caused by physical abuse, alcoholism, or marital strife. In the popular press, a nuclear family with children, based on love and mutual respect, was seen as ideal, although beneath the surface sex roles and the concept of marriage were changing rapidly.

During the 1960s, birth control, the sexual revolution, and the Vietnam War caused an entire generation of young people to question authority.[109] Borrowing from the civil rights movement and anti-war demonstrations, the women's liberation movement attacked the institution of marriage, lamented the oppression of women, and sought alternatives to traditional marriage through education, careers, and equal rights for women.

New Marriage Norms

It took decades for our current ideas about marriage and divorce to develop. During the 1970s and 80s, women changed their attitudes toward work and marriage after becoming educated and beginning careers or getting divorced. Women's expectations for fulfillment within marriage were often unmet, and they began looking for alternatives. The transformation began in the 1960s, when mothers encouraged their daughters to get educated, start careers, and postpone marriage.[110] Young men had their own concerns about traditional marriage, believing that supporting a family was financially burdensome. Many were not ready to commit to one woman after the sexual revolution made premarital sex readily available.

When women went to work after the war, they viewed their income as a supplement until they married, became pregnant, and started their families. Once they had children, married women generally quit work, and only some returned to it after their children were grown. As women became better educated and new career opportunities opened for them, young women changed their attitudes toward work and marriage. Educated women wanted careers first and perhaps marriage or family later. As their expectations increased and women became economically independent, divorce rates soared. With the discovery of effective birth control, women were able to reliably separate sex from childbearing. Many women opted for childless marriages, placing more pressure on the institution. Women raised their expectations for marriage to the point where they became difficult to fulfill. The result was fewer marriages, lower rates of reproduction, higher divorce rates, and digital dating.

Online Dating

The internet is transforming how people find mates.[111] Over 200 million individuals use digital dating services every month. For centuries people found a marriage partner through family connections, school, work, or among their friends. Today, internet dating offers another option for finding a mate. However, some men have difficulty finding a mate on the internet, because men and women express interest in members of the opposite sex at very different rates: men want to meet around 60 percent of the women they see online, while women are interested in meeting under 6 percent of the men available online. Marriages made online are turning out to be slightly more stable and happier than marriages created the old-fashioned way. And digital dating has special appeal to individuals with unique mating requirements, such as religious restrictions or same-sex preferences. Over 70 percent of gay couples meet online, because it's safer and they can be certain the other person has a similar sexual orientation.

There are negative aspects to online dating, however. Feedback can be brutal when people make snap judgments about the attractiveness of someone they have never met. Digital dating is associated with significant depression among the minority of participants who aren't successful at finding a mate. As well, it's estimated that over 10 percent of profiles on the internet don't belong to real people.

Digital dating allows individuals to choose partners like themselves and increases assortative mating based on education, social class, and income. Someday we may even see genomes displayed on digital dating profiles, so a person will be able to choose a mate with the genetic characteristics preferred for his or her children. Millions are finding mates online, and there are sites for many different preferences, including sites for finding more than one partner at a time and for other unusual sexual preferences.

How does age affect the desirability of males and females in online dating? Research has found that female desirability on the internet is highest at around age eighteen years and drops with increasing age, while male desirability begins low, reaches a peak at around fifty years, and then falls gradually as men age. However, men in their sixties are as desirable as women in their thirties for online dating. Postgraduate education is a plus for men and a negative for women in online dating. As you might expect, companies are using the data they collect to train algorithms to make online matches more accurate.

Dual career marriages are the new way to get ahead financially.

Family Finances

A major force driving women into the labor market is family finances. In the nineteenth century, there were three ways for a family to advance economically. One was to send their children out to work, another was for the family to move from a farm to the city, and the third was for the husband to invest in more education and get a better-paying job. Child labor laws abolished the opportunity for children to work outside the home by the turn of the century, and after the Second World War the majority of families had migrated to cities. By the 1970s, additional education offered diminishing financial returns for many husbands. As these older strategies for getting ahead disappeared, a working wife became the new avenue for family economic progress.

As baby-boom couples are aging and their children leaving home, more of them are getting divorced than ever, creating a flood of gray divorces. The divorce rate among Americans over 55 years is growing rapidly.[112] The causes of gray divorce likely include increased life expectancy, more women working outside the home, and higher marriage expectations. Baby-boomers can expect to live an average of twenty years longer than earlier generations, and they want to enjoy their golden years. As they reach retirement, and because there is little stigma to getting divorced, more and more baby-boomers are untying the knot. Most gray divorces are not marked by serious discord. Instead, older divorcing couples report that they have simply drifted apart. Most often it is the wife who files for divorce.

Experts are not certain why educated women initiate around 90 percent of divorces in their families, but they have some ideas. One theory is that educated women's expectations for marriage have increased dramatically. These women want their spouses to be their best friends and their marriage relationship to be a major source of happiness. When their husbands can't meet these heightened expectations, they divorce them. Also, because baby-boomers are older and have accumulated more assets, it's easier for them to divorce, because there's generally enough money for both spouses to survive. Their children are grown, and they can be financially independent and autonomous.

Another cause of gray divorce is adultery. Baby boomers came of age during the sexual revolution and experienced more sexual partners prior to marriage than did earlier generations. These early sexual experiences appear to have given them a taste for sexual variety, leading to higher rates of adultery. The sense of betrayal when spouses are found cheating often leads to divorce. Older divorced men and women have more options, with online dating sites specifically designed for them and the stigma of cohabitation largely a thing of the past. Older men and women no longer need to stay married for fear of social rejection. For older individuals in good health, with adequate financial resources, a gray divorce can mean freedom, independence, and personal fulfillment. However, if older men or women are in poor health, with limited resources, divorce can plunge them into poverty and despair.

Not only are older couples changing their ideas about marriage, so are their adult children.

New Marriage Norms

Young Americans are postponing marriage, rejecting casual sex, and cohabiting more frequently. The risk of sexually transmitted diseases and the turmoil of promiscuous sex have made casual sexual relationships less attractive to younger generations, so the opportunity to live with one partner has become more appealing. Rather than forming traditional marriages, however, many young people are opting for living together without marriage, choosing trial marriage, or having children out of wedlock.[113] Many of these couples don't marry even after they have children. Moreover, it's no longer necessary to marry before getting a job or being active socially. Most young people believe that a "good" marriage is desirable, but their expectations have changed. For many young Americans, getting married is less important to social and economic status than it was a generation ago. Today young people can get jobs, go to parties, earn a good living, and have children without being married or even living together.

Many men wonder why they should get married at all, when sex is readily available. Young women ask why they should have to put up with a husband to have children, when they are working and can afford to support themselves and their children without a mate. Surprisingly, many young people are having less sex than their parents did. The most likely reason is that married couples have more sex than singles, and many young people are not marrying. Also, the Great Recession of the late 2000s created economic stress for many young people, and they can't afford to date as often or have sex. Another possible reason is that men's social skills have eroded because they spend so much time playing video games rather than being socially active. The answers to these questions will have major implications for American society in the coming years.

Chapter 7

History of Divorce

Among early hunter-gatherer couples where sex roles were roughly equal, divorce was probably informal and fairly frequent. We have no written records of family relationships among our ancient ancestors, so it's difficult to be certain of their mating and divorce practices. Experts speculate that tribal customs and family beliefs governed mating and divorce among ancient tribes, that hunter-gatherer chiefs may have selected mates to enhance their power and social status, that leading families may have managed mate selection for their children, and that most individuals probably mated and separated according to taste, opportunities, and the fortunes of war. Later in our evolutionary history, divorce among agricultural and herding communities was governed by formal written laws or religious doctrines as societies became more settled, organized, and complex. Divorce occurs in most societies. Only the Philippines, the Vatican City, and the British Crown Dependency of Sark don't allow divorce.[114]

Some of our earliest records of divorce are from ancient China.

Divorce in China

Ancient Chinese society discouraged divorce, although it was available on restricted grounds to couples willing to endure the stigma. There were three ways to dissolve a marriage in ancient China: no-fault divorce by mutual consent, state-mandated annulment of the marriage, and a husband's divorce of his wife with cause. Ancient Chinese law allowed a couple to divorce by mutual consent because of incompatibility. The only formal requirement was that the husband write a note stating he was divorcing his wife. Chinese marriages were annulled if a wife committed a serious crime against her husband or his family. Finally, a husband could divorce his wife for a lack of filial piety toward his parents, failing to bear a son, adultery, gossiping, contracting a disease, or committing theft.

After the Chinese Communists gained power in 1949, liberal family laws were introduced, and women were permitted to divorce their husbands without their consent.[115] These new divorce laws triggered some murders of young women who attempted to divorce their traditional, rural husbands. During the early years of communist rule divorce was rare, but it has become more common in larger cities recently. Most Chinese marriages are dissolved because of adultery. Divorce is also available on grounds of bigamy, domestic violence, drug addiction, separation for more than two years, and mutual alienation of affection. Increasing divorce rates are causing concern within the Chinese government. To lower the rate, marriage counselors are being trained to "fix" broken marriages. A Chinese man cannot divorce his wife if she is pregnant or within a year after she gives birth, but Chinese women can get a divorce even when they are pregnant.

Divorces have become more frequent in China because the process is easy, women are better educated or employed, and adultery has increased. The divorce rate is higher in Chinese cities compared with rural areas, approaching 25 percent in the larger cities. The overall divorce rate in China is about one fourth the rate in America (nearly 13 percent).[116] Chinese men usually gain custody of their children following a divorce, and divorced women have trouble finding a job. Spying on a spouse is encouraged in China, and many divorces are triggered when a person discovers adultery or a crime being committed by his or her spouse.

Divorce laws were liberal in Ancient Rome.

Divorce in Ancient Rome

The earliest recorded case of marriage dissolution in Rome occurred when a citizen divorced his wife because she was unable to bear children. The government required him to divorce his barren wife and marry another woman in order to produce Roman citizens. This was certainly not the first Roman divorce, because men could divorce their wives for drinking wine, going to public places of entertainment without consent, and other acts of moral perversity. A Roman husband had no duty to support his wife after a divorce for cause. Once Roman women gained the right to own property, they could also sue for divorce.

Marriages between Roman citizens were private partnerships, formed by mutual consent and based on affection or social, political, and financial gain. If affection turned to indifference, Roman couples could divorce by giving formal notice in writing, similar to modern no-fault divorce.[117] Roman law did not require a judicial inquiry unless the spouses couldn't agree about divorce terms.

An ancient Roman divorce petition had to be formalized in writing, signed by the divorcing party, and delivered to his or her spouse in the presence of witnesses. Generally, the terms of divorce were that each spouse would keep his or her own property, while the children would remain with their father. Roman courts looked for fault if they became involved in a divorce and the couple couldn't agree about terms. If a spouse was guilty of perverse morals, the courts could require him or her to forfeit property to the innocent spouse. Roman courts also exercised jurisdiction over children when the divorce was contested, deciding where they should live and often requiring both parties to contribute to the children's support. If the parties were equally guilty of moral perversity, the courts generally left each in possession of his or her own property and divorced them.

Ancient Roman laws and customs governed marriage and divorce for centuries, even after Catholicism became the official religion of Rome. Christian leaders believed marriages were ordained by God and divorce was immoral, because it contradicted basic articles of Catholic faith.[118] Catholic scholars argued that celibacy was a superior spiritual state compared with marriage, but they believed it was better to be married than to commit fornication. Remarriage after divorce was discouraged.

Allowing divorce on grounds of adultery created a paradox for Catholic women, because if they divorced a husband for his sexual misbehavior and then remarried, they became guilty of adultery themselves!

Other Catholic writers believed a husband should be able to divorce his wife for adultery but that a wife had no right to the same remedy. St. Augustine considered whether spouses should have the right to divorce on grounds of adultery, but he ultimately decided that the only way to resolve the myriad Biblical issues of marriage and divorce was to declare marriage indissoluble and divorce unavailable to Christians.

After the adoption of Christianity as the official religion of Rome, there was competition between emperors and popes over who had the right to control marriage and divorce. Early Roman emperors upheld the right to divorce, but Church authorities worked to restrict the availability of marriage dissolution. Catholic authorities based their opposition to divorce on the Bible and the rights of children to a safe and happy home. In this struggle between secular rights and church dogma, the people had little voice. Charlemagne introduced stricter divorce laws in the Holy Roman Empire during the ninth century in return for papal blessing of his divine right to rule.[119] During the fifteenth century, Catholic authorities finally decreed that marriage was indissoluble. Christian doctrine had a strong influence on divorce throughout Europe after the Middle Ages.

Divorce in the Middle Ages

During the eleventh century, Pope Gregory VII excommunicated all Eastern Orthodox Christians, because he was in competition with the Eastern pope for control of the church. Two systems of marriage and divorce developed in Eastern and Western Europe as a result. The Eastern Orthodox Church never adopted the view that celibacy was the preferred way of life for Christians; Eastern Orthodox priests were allowed to marry. Divorce continued to be available in Eastern Europe, and Orthodox bishops retained exclusive jurisdiction over divorce, which required a trial before a church authority. The Eastern episcopal courts allowed divorce on grounds of impotence, attempted murder of one's spouse, long absence, abortion, taking of monastic vows, treason, adultery, and religious differences between the spouses.

As the authority of Western Roman emperors declined relative to that of the pope, church leaders extended their control over marriage and divorce. Even strong emperors such as Charlemagne and William the Conqueror turned control of marriage and divorce over to the pope, in return for papal blessings of their divine right to rule. Gradually the Catholic Church gained authority over the daily lives of citizens, and canon laws governed marriage, divorce, and the writing of wills. Bishops who bought their agency were given the power of excommunication to enforce their rulings. Priests who were sworn to celibacy made judgments about their flock's sexual problems and often found their power quite profitable if, for example, a wealthy family wanted to resolve a marital dispute by buying an annulment.

Catholic clergy developed ways to dissolve unhappy marriages other than through divorce. The most frequent method was judicial separation, because once the spouses were legally separated, the church paid little attention to what they did. If they remarried or lived in adultery, that was considered a lesser sin and could be handled by penance. The discretion of the pope over marriages and divorce was practically unlimited, and the church allowed rich and powerful members to annul marriages and even remarry within the church—for a fee. During the Inquisition, a husband or wife could obtain a divorce by accusing his or her spouse of heresy. Since the accused individual was almost always put to death, this effectively gave the accusing spouse a divorce.

Alternatives to Divorce

One way to end a Catholic marriage was to take a vow of chastity, which dissolved the bonds of matrimony. Catholic marriages were not valid until consummated, so if the husband was impotent, the marriage could be declared void. The remedy became known as a declaration of nullity, on the ground that the marriage had never been consummated. If there were children from the marriage (how that could happen without consummation of the marriage isn't exactly clear—perhaps through adultery?), they were considered illegitimate! Another basis for declaring a marriage void was the spouses being related within the fourth degree. These strictures could be avoided by purchasing dispensations from the church. The sale of dispensations became a lucrative practice among the clergy and a source of revenue for the church, which could not levy taxes directly. These sales helped trigger the Protestant Reformation.

A typical case of annulment on grounds of consanguinity was the marriage of the Earl of Bothwell, who wanted to shed his wife and wed Mary, Queen of Scots.[120] The earl was able to find an ancestor who had married into his wife's family a century before, and an annulment was granted by the church. Perhaps the most famous annulment was when Henry VIII petitioned the pope to void his marriage to Catherine of Aragon. Henry eventually established the Church of England to replace Catholicism in his country, because the pope would not grant him serial annulments. Financial scandals triggered a break within the Christian church by Martin Luther during the Reformation.

The Reformation

The Protestant Reformation was partly a reaction to the financial excesses of the Catholic Church. Among other things, Martin Luther objected to the lucrative dispensations and indulgences bishops and the pope offered wealthy families to avoid restrictions on misbehavior, divorce, and remarriage within the church. In 1517, Martin Luther attacked canon law and repudiated the idea that marriage was indissoluble.[121] He proposed that divorce should be available on limited grounds and created a religious rupture within the Christian Church that has lasted to the present day. Within a few years, Northern Germany, Switzerland, Holland, England, and the Scandinavian countries all rejected Catholic canon law and allowed divorce on limited grounds.

Protestant Reformers believed that marriage was a social contract, divorce should be available on grounds of adultery or desertion, and a judicial trial should not be required to obtain a divorce. Adultery and desertion became common grounds for divorce throughout Protestant Europe. A typical case of desertion involved a couple who were married in a Catholic country. After the husband converted to Protestantism, he fled to Holland, because he feared the Inquisition. However, his wife remained faithful to her Catholic religion, worried that her children would be raised as Protestants if she remained with her husband, and refused to accompany him to Holland. The wife received a separation from her Protestant husband on grounds of heresy, and the husband applied to the Supreme Court of Holland for a divorce on grounds of desertion. The Dutch court granted his divorce, allowed him to remarry, and ordered restoration of his property.

Even among Protestants, scripture remained the primary basis for justifying a divorce. Marriage and divorce were theological matters, and no one wanted to be called a heretic during the Middle Ages due to fear of the Inquisition. Marriage was becoming more secular, and divorce was easier to obtain, but Protestant judges trained in canon law still justified divorce on theological grounds. Any deviation from scripture was condemned. Married couples who lived apart were fined 100 florins for every month of separation, and the fine could be enforced by imprisonment. If the couple did not unite, one of the spouses could sue for malicious desertion (a crime) and obtain a divorce.

Protestant Reformers attempted to reconcile laws on marriage and divorce with the scriptures. They allowed divorce on grounds of adultery or desertion and rejected the idea that marriage was indissoluble. Judges were presumed to represent God and granted divorces on His authority. Divorce became a prosecution of one spouse by the other, much like American fault-based divorce prior to the introduction of no-fault divorce late in the twentieth century. Protestants rejected the idea that marriage was sacred, but they placed sufficient legal and procedural barriers in the path of divorce to make getting out of a broken marriage difficult and expensive.

The lot of Protestant women was little better than their status under canon law, however. A Protestant wife was expected to endure an abusive marriage, had no legal rights to her children, and was considered a minor while she was married. Only recently have women gained most legal rights.[122] Earlier, a wife had no legal personality, and her husband had the sole right to dispose of all their property, including any separate property she brought into the marriage or inherited while married. A woman was obliged to follow her husband when he moved, and if she refused, he could divorce her for desertion. If a wife committed adultery, she was believed to have harmed her husband, and he could sue for divorce and demand money damages. Under Protestant law, divorcing couples were required to prove that one of them was at fault. Not all authorities agreed with these ideas, however. Sir Thomas More wrote that English men and women should have the right to divorce by mutual consent, although this revolutionary idea was not instituted for centuries.

France made major changes in family law following the revolution.

The French Revolution

Prior to the French Revolution, divorce was essentially unavailable in Catholic France. The Revolutionists declared that marriage was a social contract that could be broken by mutual consent. A civil ceremony was required to marry, and a divorce was granted when the parties petitioned a civil court for relief. Divorces were freely granted, and the courts didn't inquire into the cause of the divorce.

When he usurped power, Napoleon ordered a committee of lawyers to draft the Napoleonic Code to govern French society.[123] Many members of the committee were trained in canon law, so they retained the requirement of a public inquiry into the causes of divorce. However, Napoleon insisted that divorce by mutual consent be available to French citizens without a trial; he believed that divorce should be private and honorable rather than public and squalid. Napoleon argued that most couples married young and often made mistakes that could be corrected by divorce. Napoleonic Law also allowed divorce on grounds of cruelty.

Divorce was complex and expensive under Napoleonic Law. The living parents of the divorcing couple were required to consent to the divorce, and the couple needed to prove they had arranged for the care and custody of their children and the division of their assets before a divorce would be granted. The divorcing parties were required to appear in court at least three times. Divorce in France was not allowed until the couple had been married two years and was forbidden after twenty years of marriage or when the wife turned forty-five years of age—even if she wanted the divorce.

Besides mutual consent, divorce under the Napoleonic code could be had on grounds of adultery, cruelty, and the commission of certain crimes by either spouse. Generally, the innocent spouse received custody of their children. The Napoleonic Code, despite its many restrictions on divorce, was a major change from canon law and the restrictive marital laws of the Reformers. Following the fall of Napoleon and the restoration of the French Monarchy, Catholic canon law was reinstated and not abolished until 1884 when the French civil code was introduced. Even then, divorce by mutual consent did not become available for decades.

English family law evolved differently.

English Divorce Law

Prior to the Norman Conquest in 1066, divorce by consent was available in Saxon England. Divorce was allowed on grounds of desertion, adultery, impotence, long absence, captivity, or incompatibility. Canon law was introduced in England by William I and displaced the ancient Saxon laws of consensual divorce.[124] Henry VIII eventually repudiated the Catholic Church and replaced it with the Church of England, when his attempt to annul his marriage to Catherine of Aragon was thwarted. Henry had married Catherine when he was a youth, and when she was unable to produce a male heir, he decided to end that marriage and take another wife to give him sons. Pope Clement VII was willing to grant the annulment, but only if Catherine would agree that her first marriage had been consummated, which she refused. Henry took matters into his own hands and commissioned the newly appointed Archbishop of Canterbury, Thomas Cranmer, to grant him a divorce. The pope excommunicated Henry and the Archbishop of Canterbury. These and other events caused a break between the Church of England and Rome, bringing the Church of England under Henry's control and initiating the English Reformation.

Henry constituted a commission to revise family law for the Church of England, authorizing divorce on grounds of adultery, desertion, long absence, cruelty, an attempt to kill a spouse, and deadly hatred between spouses. Husbands and wives were given equal rights to divorce and re-marry. However, this liberal divorce law was never passed by the English Parliament, so a modified version of canon law governed marriage and divorce in Protestant England for generations. Wealthy men were able to obtain divorces by private acts of Parliament after obtaining separations from the ecclesiastical court.[125] Parliamentary divorces were usually granted on grounds of adultery, and the parties were allowed to remarry.

The English Parliament eventually passed the English Divorce Act in 1857, giving jurisdiction over divorces to the English Supreme Court.[126] A husband could obtain a divorce on grounds of adultery and had a right to sue for damages. However, a wife could only divorce her husband if she proved adultery, desertion, cruelty, bigamy, or incest. She could not sue for damages. Despite support of women's rights by liberal writers such as Bentham and Mill, women remained second-class citizens under English divorce law for decades.

In contrast, divorce was available in several of the American colonies.

Divorce in Colonial America

The original New England colonists brought marriage and divorce laws from Protestant Holland to America because they had no state mandated church and didn't follow canon law.[127] Marriage in the New England colonies was based on a contract signed before a civil magistrate. The right to divorce was recognized, and adultery was the main basis for dissolution of a marriage, although some New England colonies also recognized desertion, cruelty, impotence, disease, or gross misbehavior as grounds for divorce. Husbands and wives were given equal rights before most colonial courts. The US Constitution acknowledged that the various states retained exclusive rights over marriage and divorce. Today, most American divorces are handled in county courts before judges.

American judges enjoy wide discretion to grant divorces, and there is no single divorce law in the United States. Instead, each state has developed its own family laws, and these may differ substantially. Even though no-fault divorce eventually became available in every state, divorced individuals were stigmatized and considered morally suspect—especially divorced women, because it was the woman's job to protect the morality of the family, and divorce was seen as an ethical and moral failure on her part.

During the 1920s, women's role in society began to change as many young educated females pursued careers rather than marriage and family.

Many of these educated women were not satisfied with the traditional role of women. They wanted economic opportunity, sexual freedom, satisfying careers, and marriage on their own terms, as we saw in the earlier chapter on feminism. Because they were already financially independent, these women didn't need husbands to support them. When they married, they intended to continue working even after starting a family. Family size was limited by increasingly available effective birth control. However, even if women worked outside the home, they were still expected to be the homemakers and caretakers of children. These expectations placed a serious burden on educated young women. Many rebelled, filed for divorce, or didn't marry at all. Although most modern marriages are performed before civil authorities, religions have had a major impact on mating and divorcing.

Chapter 8

Divorce and Religion

When humans shifted from hunting and gathering to raising crops and herding animals, fewer people were needed to produce food for the larger population. As a result, individuals specialized in protecting the city, policing the population, managing the government, and directing religious beliefs and activities. Industrialization and trade further increased the availability of goods and food, so more people shifted from farming to urban living and specialized activities. Governments levied taxes, offered protection, and regulated people's lives through civil laws, police forces, and religious institutions. Religious leaders guided the spiritual life of the people and controlled marriage and divorce in the early history of most agricultural societies.

Three major religions have influenced marriage and divorce: Judaism, Christianity (Catholicism or Protestantism), and Islam. Judaism and Christianity developed in association with the Roman Empire, while Islam developed later within the Ottoman Empire.

The Jewish religion developed first and has a long history in Western civilization.

Jewish Divorce. Early Jewish law gave husbands the exclusive right to initiate a divorce, although Jewish wives gained the right to divorce centuries later. Remarriage under Jewish law was permitted for both males and females after a divorce. Infidelity and impotence were primary causes of divorce among Jews. [128] Joseph considered divorcing Mary when she became pregnant because he had not consummated their marriage and believed she had been unfaithful. Church doctrine holds that Joseph was dissuaded from divorce by an angel who informed him of the true facts about Mary's situation. A Jewish husband could not divorce his wife unless his accusation of adultery was proved. Jewish women obtained the right to file for divorce in the eleventh century. Under later Talmudic law, a Jewish woman could divorce her husband if he was impotent, if he falsely accused her of adultery, if he had a disease, or deserted her. Catholic doctrine ultimately outlawed dissolution of marriage among Christians.

Catholic Doctrine

Catholic authorities followed Roman practices for centuries but eventually insisted that all Catholic priests be celibate.[129] Catholic doctrine taught that sex within marriage was acceptable for procreation only. Christ asserted that "whosoever shall put away his wife, and marry another, committeth adultery." The Catholic doctrine of marriage indissolubility was a radical departure from early Roman law. Before Catholicism was established as the state religion, divorce was readily available throughout the Roman Empire on grounds of adultery, procuring, or poisoning, in the case of husbands, and on grounds of homicide, poisoning, or violating graves for wives. Divorce remained available under the Catholic Church until the Middle Ages.

St. Augustine suggested that the innocent party who divorced his or her adulterous spouse should be allowed to remarry, because the adulterer should be considered civilly dead according to the Biblical injunction that adulterers must be stoned to death. Other Catholic authorities also argued that an innocent spouse should be allowed to remarry after a divorce for adultery, but Catholic authorities eventually decreed that marriages could only be ended by annulment.[130]

Once Roman Emperor Constantine converted to Christianity in the fourth century, early Christian emperors and popes began restricting the rights of Roman women to divorce and limiting the grounds for divorce. For several centuries divorce by mutual consent was still allowed, but if a divorce was not by mutual consent, the parties were required to file in a civil court. Under Justinian Law, women could file for divorce if their husbands committed adultery in the same town where the couple lived, or if the husband committed murder, fraud, sacrilege, or treason. However, Roman women couldn't divorce their husbands simply because they were abusive. Catholic doctrine has influenced European divorce laws since at least the Middle Ages.

Under later canon law, dissolution of a marriage could only be done by annulment for just cause.

Annulment

Annulment is not the same as divorce, because when a marriage is annulled, it is deemed to never have existed.[131] In contrast, a divorce dissolves a valid marriage. Annulments were granted under arcane interpretations of Catholic canon law, by discovering technical impediments to the existence of the marriage. Annulments could be granted for marriage defects discovered at a later date. Many authorities believe annulments were used to free wealthy or powerful individuals from unwanted marriages and were simply an expedient way to avoid the indissolubility of Catholic marriage. Canon law contained several impediments to a valid marriage, including consanguinity or affinity (genetic or marital relationships that barred marriage).

These prohibitions were sometimes carried out to the fourteenth degree to find an impediment and annul a marriage for a wealthy or powerful family. This meant, for example, that a marriage was not valid if the man and woman were sixth cousins or closer in familial relationship. Most often the prohibition to a valid marriage was only carried to the fourth degree to find a useful impediment and allow annulment. Consanguinity or affinity were the favorite ways to justify annulment of an inconvenient marriage.

Another impediment to a valid marriage was spiritual, such as when the person who married a couple had participated in his or her own baptism. Also, girls could not legally marry before twelve years or boys before fourteen years of age. If a male was impotent, that was a bar to a valid marriage, because the relationship could not be consummated. Consent was necessary for a valid Catholic marriage, so insanity and the resulting inability to give informed consent was an impediment that could lead to an annulment.

Protestant Reformers believed annulments were often granted on technical grounds as a substitute for divorce, and they passed more liberal divorce laws as a concession to religious and judicial honesty. It must be noted that annulments were not a frequent way to end marriages during the Middle Ages in Catholic countries, because they were mainly available to wealthy or powerful families who could afford the fees.

In addition to annulments, some Catholic couples were allowed to separate to preserve family peace.

Judicial Separation

Known formally as "separation from bed and board," Catholic judicial separation was based on some offense by one spouse against the other that made living together impossible.[132] Judicial separation did not dissolve a Catholic marriage, but the separated individuals were not obligated to live together. Even though they lived in separate houses and maintained separate economic accounts, the couple was expected to be sexually faithful so long as they lived, although this stricture was often ignored. A legally separated individual could not marry another person until his or her spouse died, and then it was as a widow or widower rather than as a single person. Voluntary unauthorized separations were considered a sin under canon law, whether they took place by desertion or mutual consent, although informal separations certainly happened.

Judicial separations did not end the marriage bond or declare the marriage invalid. Instead, they reduced the obligations of the spouses toward each other. They were granted for extreme cruelty, adultery, heresy (belief opposed to accepted Catholic doctrine), and apostasy (abandonment of the Catholic faith). Judicial separations were rationed because church authorities tried to keep couples in the same household with their children when possible.

During the early history of the Roman Empire, marriages were private contracts between families. When Catholicism became the official religion of Rome, canon law gradually formalized the requirements for a valid marriage and eventually awarded exclusive jurisdiction for enforcement of marriage and divorce laws to church courts. The formal basis of a valid Catholic marriage required proper consent by the spouses and being of marriageable age. Canon law undermined the power of parents and lords to control the marriages of children and serfs and awarded that power to the Catholic Church. In the eleventh century, canon law was refined, and the indissolubility of marriage became Catholic doctrine after the Council of Trent.[133] Marriage also became a sacrament (one of the Christian rites instituted by Jesus Christ to confer grace—such as baptism, confirmation, penance, and holy orders). Remarriage was generally forbidden within the church.

Remarriage

The right to remarry distinguished annulment from judicial separations in Catholic doctrine. Catholics were allowed to remarry only if their marriage had been annulled, because that meant it had never existed. Remarriage was also allowed if a spouse had died. Only a few conservative Catholic authorities held that, because marriage was indissoluble, death did not give a married spouse the right to remarry. More liberal church authorities believed remarriage should be available after a spouse died, even though church authorities didn't recommend remarriage. Since the purpose of marriage, according to the Catholic Church, was the production of children, remarriage to produce children was acceptable.

A major focus of the Catholic Church was to control reproduction. In cases where remarriage was permitted, it was based on human weakness and more frequently granted to men. Remarriage had to be preceded by a penance. Widowers were allowed to remarry a previously unmarried woman. Remarriage by a widow less than a year after her husband's death was almost never permitted by the Catholic Church, to avoid confusion about the paternity of children and to lower the attraction of spousal murder.

There were exceptions to and evasions of these strict rules among Catholic populations. For example, marriages outside the church were not subject to canon law, even if the spouses were Catholic. Moreover, exclusive sexual relationships without marriage (essentially common-law marriages) were dissoluble outside the church, and the parties could remarry. Informal marriages were recognized in almost every European village if the couple lived together, shared daily activities, and acted as if they were a married couple. The old saying was, "Eat, drink, and sleep together seem to make a marriage." Stating "I take you in marriage" along with sexual intercourse made a marriage valid within the Catholic Church, but the marriage was indissoluble. Trial marriages occurred in many parts of Europe. Couples engaged in sexual intercourse prior to marriage with the knowledge and approval of the village and the expectation that they would eventually marry and produce children.

The Catholic Church condemned trial marriages and attempted to impose its authority on the entire population, with mixed success. Families that had controlled marriages among their children for thousands of years wanted to continue the practice, even though it conflicted with the Catholic doctrine that individual consent was essential to a valid marriage. Under earlier Roman laws of marriage and divorce, if a wife could not produce an heir, her husband was allowed to divorce her and remarry to produce offspring and continue his line.

Catholic authority over marriage and divorce gradually expanded as the church gained power in return for popes granting kings and emperors the divine right to rule, which was a blessing coveted by rulers. Before the twelfth century, there were significant divisions within the Catholic Church about the indissolubility of marriage, and it was not until the sixteenth century that these divisions were resolved at the Council of Trent, which outlawed Catholic divorce.

The Council of Trent

In 1563, the Catholic Church finally decided that all valid marriages were indissoluble. The Council also decreed that only marriages within the Catholic Church were valid, condemning Protestants who married outside the Catholic Church to hell and giving the church a monopoly over Catholic marriages. The Council of Trent also decreed that divorce could not be granted for heresy or desertion, but it allowed legal separations for couples who could not live together as man and wife for various reasons. Only in the eastern parts of the Roman Empire did the possibility of divorce continue to exist for Catholics after the sixteenth century.

Within the Catholic Church there was isolated pressure to relax rules about the indissolubility of marriage. For example, Thomas More, in his book *Utopia*, dealt extensively with marriage and divorce.[134] More felt that in a society where adultery and marital unhappiness existed, divorce ought to be available to dissolve broken marriages. He believed that a Utopian should be satisfied with one spouse, but if the spouse proved difficult, the husband or wife should be free to divorce and remarry. Thomas More advocated no-fault divorce on grounds of incompatibility, a radical idea at the time.

Outside the Catholic hierarchy, opposition to the indissolubility of marriage was vigorous among Protestant Reformers.

Protestant Divorce

After Martin Luther issued his proclamations, European divorce laws began to change in Protestant countries. Few Protestants favored divorce, but they saw it as a lesser evil. Nearly all Protestant countries legalized some form of divorce by the end of the sixteenth century. Martin Luther and John Calvin had the most profound influence on divorce law among Protestants. Reformers argued that marriage was a superior state to celibacy and virginity, and they encouraged couples to marry, even the Protestant clergy. Luther drastically narrowed the impediments to marriage—including only consanguinity (genetic relationships) in the second degree, affinity (marital relationships) to the first degree, impotence, and ignorance of what constituted a valid marriage (because the persons could not give consent) as impediments to a valid marriage.

Protestant Reformers allowed marriage among the clergy, and Luther advocated sex for women in order to procreate. Calvin believed marriage was not a sacrament (a ritual that confers grace on the person), pointing out that marriage existed among nonbelievers as well as Catholics. Both Luther and Calvin embraced the concept of divorce under certain conditions, including desertion, incompatibility, impotence, the wife being unwilling to engage in sexual intercourse, inability to procreate, and adultery. They also believed marriage to be a social contract.[135] Protestant husbands were allowed to remarry under limited conditions after a divorce. Luther believed that divorce should not be easily available and that no spouse should remarry for six months following a divorce. He believed divorce should be a last resort after all avenues of reconciliation had been explored and failed.

Calvin based his support for divorce on the Old Testament injunction that an adulterous wife should be put to death. Calvin authorized divorce because historically adulterers were stoned to death, and that would end the marriage. Calvin also recommended that divorce be made available in cases of religious differences between the spouses or for desertion. Wives were not allowed to leave cruel husbands unless they feared for their lives. King Henry VIII tried to liberalize English family law after he broke with the Catholic Church, but the English Parliament didn't pass the liberal divorce laws he proposed.

Some Anglican authorities didn't adhere to the doctrine that marriages were indissoluble. They argued that desertion and adultery should remain valid grounds for divorce in England, although their views didn't gain acceptance until decades later.

The third major religious influence on marriage and divorce comes from Islam.

Islamic Divorce

According to the Koran, marriage should be based on love, and important decisions should be made by mutual consent. When there is discord within a marriage, the Koran advises spouses to divorce, although the decision should not be taken lightly and the couple should attempt reconciliation first.[136] Once a divorce is initiated, the couple is required to wait three months before finalizing it. The Koran gives a woman more rights within marriage and divorce than earlier Arab practices, such as the right to initiate a divorce, return of her property following divorce, requirement of a compelling reason before a divorce is granted to a husband, protection against unfounded accusations of adultery, and obligation for the husband to be financially responsible for his divorced wife. The Koran also creates a dowry, which becomes the property of a wife if she is divorced or her husband dies.

Muslim divorces are handled by judges drawn from the local community. They attempt to follow Islamic law, but their primary goal is to ensure harmony within the community. Spouses argue their cases before the court without attorneys. Women are allowed to appear before the court and are treated with sympathy by judges. However, a woman's testimony carries only half the weight of a man's testimony about the same matter, because women are considered lacking in rationality and self-control. Some Muslim women enter marriage with substantial property and a trousseau provided by their families, all of which has to be returned to the wife if the husband divorces her without a formal hearing. If a Muslim woman remarries following a divorce, she will generally lose custody of her children.

Marriage between a Muslim and a non-Muslim is forbidden by the Koran. Therefore, if a woman converts to Islam and her husband does not, the marriage is considered void under Islamic law and the woman receives custody of their children. Some non-Muslim women convert to Islam to get a divorce in this manner. Islamic law does not recognize community property, so assets are divided based on who brought the asset into the marriage. A husband is required to give his wife a dowry at the time of marriage, which becomes her sole property, and she is free to use the money as she wishes. The size of a dowry is associated with the status and wealth of the groom. Although some areas of Islamic law have evolved toward Western practices over the last century, the laws governing marriage and divorce have changed little over the centuries.

Marriage and divorce in the American colonies were more liberal than in Europe and the Middle East at the time.

Divorce in the American Colonies

Many colonists who left European countries were dissatisfied with the religious doctrines of the old countries; they rejected Catholic laws on divorce and adopted more liberal rules from Protestant countries. For example, the Puritans who landed at Plymouth in 1621 came to America by way of Holland, where Calvinist divorces were available. Puritans believed marriage was a civil contract rather than a religious sacrament, and divorce was made available through secular courts.[137] Divorce laws in other English colonies allowed for annulment or legal separation on grounds of desertion, cruelty, bigamy, and adultery. Once two people were divorced, only the innocent party could remarry. Among the Middle Atlantic and Southern colonies, divorce laws generally followed Catholic doctrine.

In New York, because it was originally a Dutch colony, divorce was available on grounds of desertion or giving false witness during the marriage ceremony. Remarriage was possible following a legal divorce in New York under Dutch rule. English laws on divorce were followed in the Pennsylvania colony, so no divorces or legal separations were allowed, except on grounds of adultery. Most Southern states followed strict Catholic doctrine and held that marriages were indissoluble. Many Southern colonies didn't allow divorce until they joined the United States after the American Revolution. When the American colonies became independent, divorce became more readily available throughout the states, although the grounds varied widely. Thomas Jefferson favored the easy availability of divorce, even though he was a Virginian. In many of the new states divorce was available through the legislature or the courts. Authority over divorce gradually shifted from church courts to secular institutions in early America. In the Southern States, divorce remained an exclusive right of the legislatures until the middle of the nineteenth century after the Civil War.

Decline of Religious Influence

From the seventeenth through the twentieth century, divorce gradually became secularized, as the Protestant Reformation shifted control of marriage and divorce from religious institutions to civil authorities such as state legislatures or secular courts. By the beginning of the twentieth century, marriage and divorce were governed by civil laws in most of Europe and America. However, even today many individuals are guided by their religious beliefs about marriage and divorce, no matter what the availability of civil marriage or divorce. Between 1600 and today, church influence on political, social, and personal life gradually declined. Secularization took centuries, and the shifts occurred at different rates in different countries. Catholic nations were the most resistant to change. State institutions gradually replaced church authorities in making laws, establishing and maintaining courts, providing schools for children, managing health services, and administering social welfare programs.

In addition to shifting the control of marriage and divorce from church to secular institutions, political, social, and legal theories of marriage and divorce moved away from religious foundations toward theories based on scientific methods, economic analysis, and personal values. State legislatures and courts gradually assumed control over marriage and divorce from the seventeenth century onward. The secularization of marriage and divorce brought back many elements of early Roman law, where civil authorities regulated family affairs and religion had little control over marriage or divorce.

Grotius had no difficulty reasoning that divorce was permitted under natural law.[138] He argued that Biblical "adultery" actually encompassed several offenses against the institution of marriage that justified divorce, because the bonds of matrimony had already been broken. As natural law evolved, the grounds for divorce came to include sterility, crimes against nature, incompatibility, and mutual consent.

Chapter 9

Divorce Law

We have no records describing marriage or divorce procedures among our ancient hunter-gatherer ancestors, so we know little about their mating habits or how they separated. Evidence about the marriage and divorce practices of modern hunter-gatherer tribes and data derived from artifacts of ancient tribes give us a modest understanding of what pair-bonding and divorce practices were probably like among our ancient ancestors.[139] Authorities believe that members of early hunter-gatherer tribes formed informal marriages, produced children, and created single parent households through separation, desertion, and death.

Ancient Divorce Practices

It appears that divorce among ancient hunter-gatherer tribes was gender neutral, with men and women having roughly equal rights and obligations. Women and children collected the majority of calories from foraging, while men produced high-quality protein intermittently through hunting, so there was an economic balance between the sexes. Around eleven thousand years ago, humans began cultivating crops and managing livestock rather than foraging and hunting for food. These more efficient methods of producing food transformed nomadic tribes into stable communities with larger populations and a formal system of government that developed written laws controlling marriage and divorce.

Anthropologists believe that human pair bonding evolved because women needed men to provide food and protection during pregnancy and early childhood, while human males bonded with females for sex and to avoid the damage created by competition with other males for sexual access to females. Males generally stay in a marriage for sex, while women stay in a relationship because they need resources and protection for themselves and their children. Women with small children are less likely to divorce in modern hunter-gatherer tribes compared with women who have grown children, and authorities assume that ancient hunter-gatherer women behaved in a similar way.

Death or desertion by a father has less effect on the mortality of modern hunter-gatherer children compared with the death of a mother.[140] Generally, a modern hunter-gatherer single mother is able to feed her children by gathering eggs, roots, berries, nuts, and other items through foraging, and she can teach her children to forage for themselves as they mature. Moreover, her extended family and the tribe share meat when a hunt is successful, and she may have the help of older males and females from her extended family to feed, care for, and protect her children. Modern hunter-gather tribes allow consensual divorce and have a high divorce rate. Anthropologists believe that similar marriage and divorce patterns occurred among our hunter-gatherer ancestors.

Early Divorce Law

The earliest records of laws governing divorce are from Mesopotamia, Israel, Greece, and Rome. Written records begin with the Code of Hammurabi, created around 1764 BC.[141] If a wife was innocent but her husband left or neglected her, she had a right to take her dowry and go back to her father's house. Ancient Mesopotamian women could divorce their husbands for desertion, neglect, and incompatibility. Women in Mesopotamia could initiate a divorce by announcing their intention and presenting evidence of neglect or desertion before a court. If a wife wanted to take her dowry and return to her father's house, she had to be innocent of any marital wrongdoing.

Divorce in Mesopotamia carried a strong social stigma and was apparently rare. Couples generally stayed married, even if the union was unhappy. A woman who committed adultery was often drowned. If the husband wanted to keep his adulterous wife alive, her lover had to be spared as well—an interesting dilemma for the husband. Divorce was usually initiated by the husband, but a wife could divorce her husband for abuse.[142] The major ground for divorce by a Mesopotamian husband was infertility, but he was required to return the wife's dowry. Medical experts at the time believed it was the woman's fault if a couple was unable to conceive a child. Husbands could also divorce their wives for adultery or neglecting the home. Women who wanted to avoid a public divorce sometimes quietly deserted home, husband, and children. Men were head of the family and could divorce at will. However, women had to prove conclusively that their husbands had abused or degraded them before getting divorced. Although women were considered inferior to men, they enjoyed some rights in Mesopotamia. Women could own land, run businesses, buy and sell slaves, and initiate divorce.

Divorce laws in ancient Israel were also fairly liberal.

Divorce in Ancient Israel

Ancient Hebrew law is vague about divorce, so we don't know many details about how it was handled. Children were essential to a marriage, and if a wife was barren, her husband was allowed to take a second wife to bear him heirs.[143] A widow was encouraged to marry her husband's brother. The Jewish husband was master of his home, but a wife had the right to financial support. It was important that children be genetically related to the husband, so female adultery was punished by death under Hebrew law.

Jewish divorces were generally initiated by the husband writing a note to his wife saying he wanted a divorce. Deuteronomy 24 states that a man could write a note of divorce to his wife if he found some "indecency" in her behavior. The written note was necessary to make it more difficult to divorce a wife in a fit of anger, without taking time to consider the consequences. Indecency certainly included adultery but may have included a husband simply disliking his wife. Divorced men and women could remarry others in ancient Israel and often did. A divorced woman who married another could never remarry her husband. The marriage contract specified the wife's property rights upon divorce or her husband's death.[144] The financial obligations of the marriage contract discouraged divorce.

Divorce was also available in ancient Greece.

Divorce in Ancient Greece

Divorce in ancient Greece was easy for a man—he simply had to send his wife back to her father's house. Evidence suggests divorce was rare, however. Greek men divorced their wives primarily to make a more advantageous marriage. Adultery was grounds for divorce in ancient Greece, as in most other societies. However, a man thought twice about divorcing his wife if she brought a large dowry to the marriage; he knew he would have to return the dowry, and that could prove financially difficult. Both husbands and wives had the right to divorce their spouses in ancient Greece.[145] However, a wife had to initiate a formal proceeding and bring evidence before a court to obtain a divorce. An alternate way for a Greek wife to get a divorce was for her father to initiate the proceeding. Infertility was grounds for divorce in ancient Greece, and it was blamed on the wife. A husband was required to return the wife's dowry or pay 18 percent interest until he returned the entire dowry if he divorced her.

Ancient Roman divorce laws were most liberal.

Divorce in Ancient Rome

Marriages in ancient Rome was based on consent, so it seemed natural to Romans that they should be able to get a divorce if they wanted one. Ancient Romans could divorce by sending letters to their spouses or declaring before witnesses that they wanted to divorce.[146] Children belonged to the father, and there was no community property in Rome, so the major financial issue was what to do with the wife's dowry, which generally had to be returned if a husband initiated the divorce. A woman who brought a large dowry into a marriage had considerable power over her husband—he might face financial ruin if he initiated a divorce and had to return her dowry.

If a Roman wife initiated the divorce, her husband was allowed to keep one-sixth of her dowry for each of their children, up to three. Thus, if they had three children and the wife initiated the divorce, her husband could retain half her dowry to support their children. If the wife committed adultery, the husband could retain another sixth of her dowry in addition to the fraction for each child. Husbands could also make life miserable for their divorced wives by not allowing them to visit their children. A few women won custody of their children when the fathers were "wicked," but that was rare in ancient Rome.

The Justinian Code allowed women to divorce if they proved their husbands had plotted to murder them, whipped them, or brought prostitutes into their homes.[147] Around 421 BC, divorce in Rome was made more difficult. After that a wife had to prove her husband was guilty of vices or she had to forfeit her entire dowry in order to obtain a divorce. However, we aren't certain what actually happened in the lives of ordinary Romans. Occasionally, the way a wife's dowry was divided and who got custody and access to their children was disputed, and the issue had to be brought before a court of law for resolution, but that was rare.

Under Emperor Augustus, a husband was required to divorce his wife if she committed adultery, and she had to forfeit to him one-half her dowry and one-third of any other property she owned. Roman citizens were becoming concerned about the high incidence of divorce and its impact on children, however. During the reign of Constantine, divorce could only be obtained by a wife if she could prove that her husband was murderous, a preparer of poisons, or a disturber of tombs. Otherwise, if a wife obtained a divorce, she lost her dowry and was exiled to an island for life. A Roman husband could only divorce his wife if he proved she was an adulteress or a preparer of poisons, and he was required to return her dowry. However, if both parties consented to a divorce, these strict laws had no effect. These restrictive laws lasted only a few years and were repealed because they were unpopular with a majority of Roman citizens.

Roman divorce laws changed gradually after the introduction of Catholicism as the state religion.

Canon Law

After Christianity became the official religion of Rome, the Catholic Church began exercising authority over marriage, divorce, and inheritance. Since the Catholic Church viewed marriage as a sacred bond, divorce was gradually restricted over the centuries. In the sixteenth century, Catholic authorities declared that marriages were indissoluble at the same time the Protestant Reformation made divorce possible for many Protestants.[148]

Divorce in England was limited. Only wealthy and powerful men could get divorced until the middle of the nineteenth century, when English divorce laws were liberalized.

The English Matrimonial Causes Act

Passed in 1857, the Matrimonial Causes Act authorized secular marriage by mutual consent.[149] Since marriage was now based on a civil contract, English divorces came under the jurisdiction of civil courts. The Matrimonial Causes Act was primarily the work of Caroline Norton, who was trapped in an abusive marriage to her husband, George. Under existing English family law, George was allowed to bar his wife from her home, keep her from seeing their children, and beat her regularly. Caroline vowed to change English marriage and divorce laws to protect women like herself. English divorce law became even more liberal through common-law court decisions after the Matrimonial Causes Act was passed.

In 1923 Parliament passed a new law, making it easier to get a divorce in England if one spouse could prove adultery. In 1969 the English Parliament passed the Divorce Reform Act, allowing couples to divorce after two years of separation. In 1984 the English ban on divorce until the couple had been married more than three years was reduced to one year.

In France, Napoleon had a major impact on Western family law through his Code.

The Napoleonic Code

Up until the French Revolution, marriages in France were indissoluble and divorce was unavailable. Only annulments and judicial separations were allowed under Catholic canon law. Following the revolution, special committees passed laws displacing canon law with liberal divorce statutes. Marriage was defined as a civil contract, husband and wife were considered equals, divorce was made available to everyone, and marriage or divorce was placed under civil jurisdiction rather than being enforced through church courts. When a French couple fell out of love, they could get a civil divorce by mutual consent or on the initiative of either party. Divorce during the French Revolution was decided by a family counsel rather than a court.

When Napoleon took power, he established a commission to write a legal code based on Roman law.[150] Members of the commission were lawyers trained in canon law, so they initially made divorce unavailable to ordinary Frenchmen. However, Napoleon insisted that divorce by mutual consent be available in his code. The Napoleonic Code, ratified in 1803, allowed divorce by consent for incompatibility or cruelty and gave wives the right to initiate divorce. However, the Napoleonic Code subjugated women to their husbands within the family, and the lawyers who wrote the code retained much of canon law in their final rules.

The Napoleonic Code allowed divorce by mutual consent, but the rules and procedures for obtaining a divorce were complex, expensive, and time consuming, with the result that few French couples could afford to divorce. After the fall of Napoleon and the reinstatement of the French monarchy and the Catholic Church in 1816, canon law was reenacted. Divorce became impossible in France until 1884, when the French Civil Code was passed. Under the new French marriage laws, divorce was made available by consent, and the grounds for divorce were liberalized to include desertion, cruelty, refusal of marital rights (sexual relations), the existence of disease, refusal to support the family, refusal to be obedient, and habitual drunkenness. France liberalized marriage and divorce laws centuries after the Protestant nations of Europe did and shortly after England passed new laws on marriage and divorce.

The English colonies in America had more liberal marriage and divorce laws, even before the American Revolution.

Early American Divorce Law

Divorce in America was influenced by Protestant laws, because the English colonies had no state-sanctioned church, and many colonists had fled Europe to escape church oppression. Although divorce was available before the American Revolution, it was rare. In the city of New York, for example, there were only four recorded divorces prior to 1776. Once the colonies obtained independence, marriage and divorce laws were handled by the states rather than the national government. Most northern and middle Atlantic states slowly abolished legislative divorces and assigned all family law cases to secular civil courts, but a few southern states retained legislative divorces for decades. The grounds for divorce varied among the states, but generally included adultery, cruelty, desertion, insanity, impotence, and habitual drunkenness. Some states allowed divorce on grounds of refusal of marital sexual duties, irreconcilable differences, gross misbehavior, and family violence. However, it was not always clear whether a couple was actually married in colonial America, because there were few records.[151] Even though American divorce law allowed marriages to be dissolved, the state and children still had an interest in keeping divorce rare. Legal authorities believed that children were harmed by divorce, and research has validated this belief.

Much of American family law is based on judicial rulings later formalized by state legislatures. Canon law never became part of the United States common law, but many early American judges relied on church doctrines for their rulings. An important feature of American divorce law is the wide discretion allowed judges in interpreting statutes and granting or withholding divorces. Many American judges used their discretion to restrict divorces. Where judicial rulings made divorce difficult, husbands and wives found other ways to avoid living in difficult relationships. They informally left marriages and formed new relationships, or they found other ways of leaving broken marriages, including moving temporarily to a state with more liberal divorce laws to establish residency and file for divorce.

American family laws evolved to allow divorce based on adultery, desertion, physical abuse, impotence, insanity, or attempted murder. The result was that married individuals who wanted a divorce often colluded to establish the formal evidence required to get a divorce. A judicial inquiry would be held to confirm legitimate legal grounds for the divorce (often alleged adultery), or the divorce would not be granted, and some educated and employed women chose to remain single rather than marry.[152] In some states, the couple, or one of them, was required to remain celibate for some interval after a divorce and before he or she could remarry.

Modern Divorce Laws

Divorce laws in America became more liberal after World War II, and the incidence of divorce rose, although the rate was lower than it is today. Divorce rates generally increase following a major war. Examples include the American Civil War, WWI, and WWII.[153] Interestingly, countries that remained neutral, such as Sweden and Switzerland, didn't experience an increase in divorce rates following major world wars. The causes of increased divorce rates after a war are believed to include hasty marriages made during the war, forced separations that led to loss of love, increased likelihood of adultery when spouses were in different countries, and a natural correction of the lower divorce rates that occur during war years, when couples who would have divorced but for the war ended their marriages when the conflict was over.

Divorce laws in American are complex. A few states, such as Nevada, Idaho, Florida, and Arkansas, liberalized their divorce laws early and lowered their residency requirements to as little as six weeks to qualify for a divorce. The reward for liberalizing their divorce laws was increased economic activity from Americans seeking a quick and easy dissolution of their marriages in a divorce-mill state. By 1940, the divorce rate in Nevada was the highest in the United States, with Florida close behind. Miami and Las Vegas were the divorce capitals of America at the time.[154]

Some populous states, such as New York, had restrictive divorce laws that required finding fault before a divorce could be granted. Couples who didn't want to commit perjury by confessing to adultery in court moved to Nevada or Florida to get a divorce after establishing easy residency. By moving to Nevada for a few weeks, a couple could get a divorce and move back to New York as single individuals, because all states must respect the laws of other states. Other people moved to France for a divorce under that country's liberal laws. The most popular American divorce location, however, was Chihuahua, Mexico, just across the border from Texas. Chihuahua's laws allowed divorce for incompatibility, and residency could be established the day you arrived in Mexico, so there was no waiting for a Mexican divorce. After decades of watching migratory divorce or perjury before American family-law judges, some state legislators decided it was time to change their family laws by introducing no-fault divorce laws into their statutes.

No-Fault Divorce

The first modern no-fault divorce laws were passed in the Soviet Union in 1917 after the Communist Revolution. Communist authorities transferred jurisdiction over divorce from church to state courts and allowed divorce at the request of either spouse. California passed the first American no-fault divorce law in 1969, allowing dissolution on grounds of irreconcilable differences based on written assertions by the couple.[155] By 1977, nine states had adopted no-fault divorce laws, and by 1983 every state except South Dakota and New York allowed no-fault divorce. Finally, in 2010, New York became the last state to pass a no-fault divorce law.

Critics of no-fault divorce argue that it increases the incidence of divorce, ruins families, and harms children. Studies into the effects of no-fault divorce typically find a short-term increase in the divorce rate following passage of no-fault divorce laws in a state but little long-term change in divorce rates. Studies have also found that domestic violence and spousal suicide decline following the passage of no-fault divorce laws, which are certainly good outcomes. Blaming no-fault divorce laws for the high rate of divorce in America is too simplistic. There are many factors associated with high divorce rates besides liberal laws. Stephanie Coontz found that following the introduction of no-fault divorce the natural rate of American divorce stabilized at around seventeen per thousand in 2005.[156]

The National Organization of Women opposed the introduction of no-fault divorce in the United States, because they believed it would allow husbands who committed adultery to avoid the consequences of their actions when a judge set alimony, child support, and decided on a division of marital property. However, that didn't happen, because many states allowed a divorcing spouse to plead and prove fault in a divorce and thus receive a larger share of the community estate and alimony. Other experts argued that no-fault divorce could condemn many women with children to poverty or allow women to take children from the husband through no fault on his part. However, it's unclear whether no-fault divorce increased the incidence of divorce, because we can't measure the natural rate of broken marriages independently of the divorce rate.

The "Natural" Divorce Rate

When trying to understand the "natural" rate of divorce, it's important to understand the difference between the incidence of marriage breakdown and the incidence of divorce. The "natural" divorce rate is a complex function of the number of broken marriages in a population, the available grounds for divorce, the cost of getting a divorce, the social stigma associated with being divorced, religious beliefs, and economic conditions. Therefore, it's not surprising that the "natural" rate of divorce didn't change dramatically following the passage of no-fault divorce laws, because there are many other factors involved that didn't change at the same time. The legal system and the grounds available for divorce are not the primary reasons couples decide to divorce or stay married. More important causes of divorce include emotional and economic factors.

Chapter 10

Economics of Divorce

Both marriage and divorce involve economic issues.[157] For generations, families negotiated the terms of marriages, including support for the wife and children, paying a dowry or bride-price, and transferring ownership of assets at marriage, divorce, and death. In earlier generations, the conditions for dividing property following divorce were generally stated in the marriage contract, similar to the modern prenuptial agreements used by wealthy individuals to protect their separate property in the event of divorce. Today, civil laws govern the division of assets, alimony, and child support in divorces. Traditionally, when women brought a dowry to the marriage, the rules varied about who owned these assets, based on where the couple lived and the terms of their marriage contract, but marriage has always involved property rights.[158] Men and women have had different economic roles in marriage.

Gender Roles

Throughout history, men and women have assumed specialized roles in the economic life of the family. During ancient times, when groups of men hunted for meat while women and children gathered fruit, nuts, roots, eggs, and other foods from the land, both tasks were essential to survival, so gender roles were roughly equal among our ancient ancestors. If a hunter-gatherer couple separated or the husband died, the single mother and her children would usually be protected by her family and the tribe.

She and her children could gather food, and successful hunting groups shared meat with the entire clan. Therefore, a divorced or widowed mother and her children were fairly certain to survive without the support and protection of a husband and father.

When humans began farming and raising livestock, men generally owned the land, plowed the fields, and managed the herds, while women grew fruits, vegetables, and nuts for the table, harvested, cooked, and cared for children and the household. When towns and cities began to grow, small businesses were opened and run by families, with the husband, wife, and children working together to earn a living. Divorce rarely happened in these families, because both husband and wife were essential to maintaining the farm or business. These marriages were mainly economic partnerships designed to help the family survive, and financial pressures made divorce rare and economically destructive.

With the advent of industrialization, men began to work outside the home or farm and women specialized in caring for house and children.[159] Early in the industrial age, men, women, and children worked in factories, although the patterns of employment were different. Children worked until they grew old enough to become apprentices or housemaids or take adult factory jobs. Men continued to work, while women stayed employed until they married and then many quit working to raise their children and care for the home. When the children were grown, some women returned to work. The consequences of divorce for women with children were often catastrophic during the industrial age. They might be left with children to support, little money, and no job, while their ex-husbands could continue their prior employment and be better off financially without the burden of supporting a family. Alternatively, the husband might retain custody of his children, and the divorced wife would be alone without funds or access to her children. The economics of divorce has a long and complex history.

History of Divorce Economics

The Old Testament gave husbands the right to divorce their wives unilaterally, but they were required to support them and their children following the divorce. Talmudic law gave women the right to divorce their husbands; however, both were required to support their children. The laws of marriage and divorce have changed in more modern times due to social, economic, and political factors, but for hundreds of years divorce was nearly impossible to obtain in Catholic countries, although annulments or legal separations were available. As opportunities opened for women in the labor market, their valuation of marriage dropped compared with other options, such as education and a career.[160]

Divorce laws that required men to pay alimony and child support and to divide marital assets with their ex-spouses increased the attractiveness of divorce for many educated working women. A divorced wife could have an income from her ex-husband and primary control of their children but not have to put up with an abusive or bothersome husband. Divorce laws that gave women preference in custody of their children almost certainly contributed to the fact that over 70 percent of all divorces—90 percent of divorces among educated couples—in America are filed by women.[161] These legal and economic changes made divorce less attractive for men, but with no-fault divorce easily available, male preferences make little difference in the high rate of divorce in modern America.

Ancient Economics of Divorce

We don't know a great deal about the economic conditions of divorced Jewish women. Jewish wives had a right to financial support during the marriage. A bride-price was common in ancient Israel, and if a Jewish wife was divorced or widowed, her family received these funds to support her and the children. Divorced Jewish women could also remarry and receive support from a second husband. Jewish women were usually protected by a marriage contract which specified their property rights upon divorce or death of their husbands. Financial terms in the marriage contract generally discouraged divorce in most ancient civilizations, because they often required the husband to return significant property to the divorced wife.

In ancient Greece, divorce was readily available, but Greek men thought twice about divorcing their wives, because they were obligated to return their dowries if they initiated divorce.

In ancient Rome, children belonged to the father, and there were no community property rights. A Roman wife could only rely on the return of her dowry for support if she was divorced or widowed. Roman husbands might face financial ruin if they initiated the divorce and had to return a large dowry.

Annulments and judicial separations were allowed in Catholic Europe, so women had to be concerned about having their marriages declared invalid—they could end up with annulled marriages and no means of support. Often these women were forced to enter convents to survive. When a Catholic couple was granted a judicial separation, they were still married, so the husband was required to support his wife and their children even though they lived in separate households.

In modern times, many women face financial difficulties if they are divorced, especially if they have not worked outside the home for years.

Divorce and Income

Both men and women are generally worse off financially following a divorce. Studies show that the income of divorced women generally decreases, while the income of divorced husbands may increase following a breakup.[162] The economic consequences vary depending on whether both spouses worked outside the home. When only the husband did, his income may increase following divorce while the wife may face severe financial hardships. But if both spouses worked outside the home, a divorced husband's income usually falls, because he no longer is able to share two incomes and may have to pay alimony and child support. Divorce is a financial and emotional burden on both husband and wife, no matter whether there is one income or two. The average cost of a divorce in America is estimated at around $20,000, but many factors can affect the average cost of a divorce—including the reasonableness of the clients, the complexity of the case, and how much they want to fight.[163]

Divorce can be an economic disaster for the entire family. Both husband and wife suffer financial stress when they divorce, because they must pay two mortgages, two sets of utility bills, etc., increasing costs for both spouses. Basic expenses increase while incomes remain essentially the same. Studies show that on average single-mother households have lower incomes compared with single-father households following divorce. Additionally, family debt is higher and income lower in single-parent homes with children compared to married couples with a similar number of children. Most studies find that women suffer financially more than men following divorce, and single mothers rely more heavily on government support for basic survival compared with single fathers.

There are two types of divorce laws in America.

Community Property and Common Law

American divorce laws divide into two main categories, based on whether they follow English Common Law or Spanish Community Property Law.[164] The major difference between states that follow the English Common Law and states that follow the Spanish Community Property Law involves how assets are divided during a divorce. Under English Common Law, assets owned at the time of divorce are awarded to the person who holds title to the property. For example, if a husband and wife buy a car and take title in her name, the wife will get the car after a divorce. In contrast, under Community Property laws, all assets owned at the time of divorce are presumed to be community property, and the spouse who claims an asset as his or her separate property must prove the claim by showing that the property was acquired before marriage or by gift or inheritance during the marriage.

Common Law. English common law makes it relatively easy to divide assets at divorce–all the court needs to do is look at how title is held and award the asset to the person listed as the owner. Assets such as furniture, clothing, pots and pans that have no title are generally awarded to the person who used the item or the assets are divided equitably between the husband and wife. If both parties jointly hold title to an asset, such as the family home, it's either sold and the proceeds divided fairly between them or one spouse buys the asset from the other spouse. Assets inherited or received as a gift are generally titled in the name of the person who received the inherited or gifted asset and awarded to them on divorce.

Community property laws are more complex.

Community Property Law. In those states that follow Spanish community property law (Arizona, California, Idaho, Louisiana, Nevada, New Mexico, Texas, Washington, and Wisconsin), all assets owned by the parties at the time of divorce are presumed to be community property unless proved to be separate property by clear and convincing evidence. Separate property includes assets owned before marriage; property acquired during marriage by gift or inheritance; property purchased with separate funds; capital gains on separate property; personal injury awards, except for lost wages; and property partitioned by a written marital agreement. All other assets acquired during marriage are considered community property, including salary, wages, income from separate property, pension plans, closely held businesses, professional practices, assets acquired with community funds, and assets acquired with community credit.

Property is characterized as community or separate when title is acquired. If a wife's separate funds are used to purchase a home, it's her separate property, even if acquired during the marriage. This is true even if community funds are used to pay the mortgage or make improvements on the wife's separate property home. The community estate might make a claim of reimbursement for community funds used to pay down the mortgage on a separate property home, but the house would remain the separate property of the wife upon divorce. A husband whose name is on the title as joint owner could argue that the wife gifted half of the house to him at the time of purchase. However, if she disputes that claim, the husband is likely to lose his right to half the house, unless he can show clear tangible evidence that his wife actually intended to give him a gift of half the home, such as a letter or other written evidence of a gift.

Property retains its original classification even if transformed from real estate to cash in a community property state. All assets bought on credit during marriage are presumed to be purchased with community credit, but a spouse can overcome this presumption by showing that the creditor agreed to look only to the separate credit of one spouse or that the couple agreed to use the separate credit of only one spouse for the purchase. Most income from separate property earned during the marriage is community property, with two exceptions: the spouses may agree in writing that this rule doesn't apply to the income from separate property, and income from a gift by one spouse to the other remains separate property.

There are several ways to change the character of property. For example, spouses can transform community property into separate property by executing a postnuptial agreement. And separate property may be transformed into community property by commingling community and separate funds in a single account—unless the owner of the separate funds can trace the separate funds into and out of the joint community account by clear and convincing evidence. To maintain the character of separate property, it's best to keep separate assets segregated in a different account from community property.

If a trust was established by the parents of the husband or wife, the principal of the trust fund is separate property, while income earned by the trust fund *and* distributed during marriage becomes community property. Oil and gas interests have the same character as the surface interest of the land that produces the oil and gas. Thus, if the land is separate property, so are the oil and gas interests. Extracting oil and gas is considered a depletion of the land, so the income derived from oil and gas production is characterized as a return of capital used to buy the land when it was originally acquired. Royalty and bonus payments also belong to the owner of the separate property land. However, rental payments are community property, because they maintain an operator's right to drill for oil and gas and are not a direct payment for extraction of minerals from the land.

The character of property and fault in the marital dissolution are important in community-property states when assets are divided during a divorce.

Division of Assets

Community-property state courts must divide marital property in a "just and right" manner during a divorce.[165] That doesn't necessarily mean a 50/50 split, because there are several factors that courts may consider in awarding one spouse a larger share of the marital estate. Even though Texas awards "no-fault" divorces, if one spouse commits adultery, family violence, a felony, or abandonment of the marriage, courts may award a larger share of community property to the innocent spouse.

Courts may consider several factors in deciding to award one spouse a larger share. For example, if the wife earns $350,000 annually while her spouse is a househusband with no employment experience, he will likely receive a larger share of the community estate during the divorce, because his wife has the ability to earn a large income following the divorce while he does not. Judges may award a larger share of the community estate to an older spouse, one who has health issues, or one who cared for their children and didn't work outside the home but has been married for a long time. Some courts give earning capacity, age, health, and length of marriage extra weight in deciding how to divide a community estate.

Most judges will award a larger share of the community estate to a spouse who has been caring for children rather than working full time during a long marriage; they believe a spouse should be compensated for his or her non-financial contribution to the family estate. Courts also consider the welfare of children when dividing property, so the spouse who receives custody of minor children may be awarded a larger share of the community estate, because child support doesn't necessarily cover all the expenses of rearing older children. Courts often punish a spouse who has wasted community assets by spending them on a girlfriend, awarding him a smaller share of the community estate. And if a spouse has committed fraud by hiding community assets, courts often award the innocent spouse a larger share of the marital estate as compensation.

Alimony

Texas courts can order the payment of spousal maintenance after a divorce but not alimony. However, a couple can agree to contractual alimony payments, and the courts will generally approve the agreement as part of a divorce settlement. Spousal support is ordered by Texas courts to provide employment rehabilitation to a spouse following divorce, so he or she can acquire education or job training and earn a living. To receive spousal maintenance a person must prove he or she is a spouse and lacks sufficient property and income to provide for minimum reasonable needs after the divorce. A spouse can also receive spousal maintenance if he or she was a victim of family violence, is disabled, or has custody of a disabled child. To be eligible for spousal support, a person must prove he or she lacks the skills to earn sufficient income for self-support and has made diligent efforts to find gainful employment or develop sufficient skills to earn a living. To receive spousal maintenance for family violence, the violent spouse must have been convicted or given deferred adjudication for family violence against his or her spouse or a family member within two years prior to the divorce.

Contractual alimony may be agreed upon between the parties and can be in any amount and for any duration. In contrast, the amount and duration of spousal maintenance is based on the needs of one spouse, the ability of the other spouse to pay, and length of the marriage. Court-ordered spousal maintenance is limited to five years for marriages over ten years, seven years for marriages between twenty and thirty years, and ten years for marriages over thirty years. Family violence spousal maintenance is limited to five years, while disability maintenance payments for a spouse or child may continue so long as the disability lasts.

Custody of Children

An important divorce issue is who gets custody of the children and receives child-support payments. Child custody can be agreed by the parents or ordered by the court. There are two types of custody: joint or sole. The major difference is who makes significant decisions about the children. In a joint custody, both parents share most rights and duties, while under a sole-custody arrangement one parent makes all major decisions involving the children. Joint custody is preferred, because it's public policy for both parents to be involved with their children. Only in cases where there's a serious problem with one spouse will a court award sole custody to the competent parent. Generally, children benefit from having contact with both parents.

There are five reasons courts may order sole custody: one parent does not want the responsibility of raising and managing his or her children; there is a history of family violence by one parent; substance abuse by one parent; criminality or abandonment by one parent; or the parents cannot agree about education, medical treatment, and religious training. Usually one parent has primary possession of the children while the other parent has visitation rights, although more couples are opting for shared custody. Standard visitation includes possessing the children on the first, third, and fifth weekends of each month, having dinner with the children on Wednesday or Thursday evenings, visits during holidays, and an extended possession period during the summer. There are special possession arrangements that can be made through a collaborative divorce, in which the parents share custody more evenly.

Child Support

Except in unusual circumstances, the parent who determines children's primary residence will receive child-support payments from the other parent.[166] The parent who has visitation rights will usually be ordered to pay child support based on his or her income and the number of children in the family. In special cases, negotiated through a collaborative divorce, the couple may reduce child support because the parents are sharing custody of the children. In this situation, child support is often calculated according to the standard formula for both parents, and the parent with the higher income pays the difference in child support owed to the parent with the lower income. Courts generally apply statutory child-support guidelines.

Texas child support is calculated by taking the paying parent's gross income and subtracting expenses to generate net income. Support payments are calculated by multiplying net monthly income by a percentage based on the number of children before the court. If one child is involved, it is 20 percent; for two children it's 25 percent; for three it's 30 percent; four children earn a percentage of 35 percent; and for five or more children, not less than 40 percent of net resources is used as the multiplier. These percentages are reduced if children from a prior marriage are concurrently receiving support. Judges sometimes order child-support payments above or below guideline amounts if it's justified by the income of both parties and the needs of the children. For example, Texas courts have approved below-guideline child support payments when the custodial parent has a much higher income than the paying parent.

Chapter 11

Causes of Divorce

Several explanations have been proposed for the high incidence of divorce in modern times, including a decline in morality, loss of religious beliefs, feminism, the employment of women outside the home, increased life expectancy, physical abuse, adultery, and higher expectations for marriage among educated women.[167] Some authorities argue that the easy availability of no-fault divorce is the primary cause of more marriage dissolutions, while others believe that most of these marriages were already broken and the current high divorce rate simply reflects the fact that many marriages are unhappy and should be ended.

Marriages can be broken and not lead to divorce if the process is expensive or unavailable because of religious or other reasons.

Marriage Breakdown and Divorce

The divorce rate and incidence of marriage breakdown are not necessarily the same. Divorce rates can be low if it's expensive and difficult to get a divorce, even though the incidence of marriage breakdown is high. This situation probably occurred during the centuries when Catholic doctrine made marriages indissoluble, the grounds for annulment or legal separation were narrow, and divorce was largely unavailable for Catholics. Later, when fault-based divorce was introduced into Protestant countries, their divorce rates increased, although it's likely that the frequency of marriage breakdowns was similar in Catholic and Protestant countries at the time.

This suggests that the availability and cost of divorce does influence the incidence of marriage dissolution but that many other factors are involved in the breakdown of marriages.[168]

When there was no provision for divorce, there was no formal dissolution of marriages, although wealthy husbands could petition the Catholic Church for an annulment or legal separation and couples deserted their marriages and informally established separate households to deal with marital breakdown. Just because there are few or no divorces in a particular country or period of history, this doesn't necessarily mean that marriages were happy in those places at that time. Marriages can break down without causing a high incidence of divorce if dissolution is expensive or unavailable. When divorce laws are liberalized, the rate of divorce increases for a while. But that does not mean liberal divorce laws *caused* the higher incidence of divorce. Instead, it's likely that many marriages were broken before liberal divorce laws were passed, and when divorce became more readily available, the unhappy couples decided to split. Generally, a short time after more liberal divorce laws are passed, the divorce rate returns to its prior level.

There are two models that attempt to explain the relationship between marriage breakdown and divorce. One theory proposes that marriage breakdown has been constant over the centuries, but divorce rates have increased in modern times because no-fault divorce became available. The other model suggests that both the number of marriage breakdowns and the divorce rate have increased over the last few centuries because of changing moral values, marital expectations, and the liberalization of divorce laws. It's difficult to determine which model is correct, because we don't know how to measure the incidence of marriage breakdown independent of the divorce rate, but it seems likely that changing moral values, rising expectations for love-based marriage, and liberalized divorce laws all contribute to the current high divorce rate.

Causes of Marriage Breakdown

The causes of divorce are complex and can be approached from legal, social, economic, or personal points of view. Divorce is a legal issue because governments have an interest in maintaining the integrity of families, safeguarding the welfare of children, and dividing marital property during a divorce. Consequently, state governments have passed laws governing the divorce process, the division of marital assets, custody and visitation of children, child support, and the availability of spousal maintenance to rehabilitate job skills or complete a person's education. Dissolution is a social issue because the changing roles of men, women, and children in modern society influence divorce rates. When women started to pursue more education and began working, they became more independent, and their expectations for marriage changed, contributing to higher modern divorce rates. Divorce is an economic issue because many women are working outside the home, so they are no longer dependent on their husbands for financial support. Marriage breakdown may happen when a spouse is addicted to alcohol, commits adultery, becomes critical, fails to support the family, or commits other destructive acts against the family.

Personal Factors. Personal factors also cause divorce: some spouses are neurotic or suffer from personality disorders. Neurotic behaviors or personality disorders create stress within a marital relationship and increase the likelihood of divorce. As well, expectations about marriage are higher today, and the stigma of divorce is lower compared with earlier generations. Consequently, many more couples are filing for divorce because they feel their marriages are not meeting their expectations, and there is little social cost to getting a divorce today.

Financial Security. Most couples expect to enjoy an appropriate standard of living after they marry, and most individuals hope their standard of living will improve following marriage. However, if a person raised in an affluent home marries someone who is neither educated nor employed, the couple's standard of living will drop dramatically, and divorce may follow.

Sexual Difficulties. Sexual availability and exclusivity are important expectations of most married couples. A modest level of adultery by a husband may be tolerated by some wives, but rarely will adultery by a wife be condoned by her husband, because it threatens his masculinity, and he does not want another man's children inheriting his assets.

In times gone by wives were considered their husbands' property, when they were bought or captured by force, or because the Bible said men should rule in the home. Some ancient societies gave men the power of life and death over their wives and children, although that was rare. For example, if a wife was guilty of adultery, her husband could have her put to death, or she could be forced to forfeit part of her dowry as compensation and he had no obligation to support her after the divorce. Children generally became the property of the husband when they were born, and women had no rights to them if the couple divorced. Modern women don't face the same hardships as their great-grandmothers, but many still feel oppressed by a male-dominated society.

Another important cause of divorce is disagreement about housekeeping and child-rearing.

Household Tasks. Many modern couples expect that household tasks and child-rearing will be shared between the spouses, but that is a relatively new idea, and many men are not accustomed to cleaning the house, taking care of children, or cooking.[169] When spouses disagree about who is responsible for these things, the issue can lead to a marriage breakdown.

Authority in The Home. Another cause of divorce is the shifting attitude toward authority within marriage. No longer is the man king of his castle. Women want more autonomy and independence within their marriage and if that is denied, they often file for divorce, especially if they are educated and employed.

The increased incidence of divorce is also caused by marriages based on romantic love—when the couple falls out of love, they often file for divorce.

Emotional Issues. The belief that romantic love is necessary for a happy marriage was a radical idea when first introduced. Throughout most of human history marriages were arranged by families for financial, social, or political reasons, with little regard for the feelings of bride or groom. Modern couples marry because of romantic love and personal characteristics of their mates and worry less about economic or social status.

Family Violence. Physical abuse is a major cause of divorce.[170] Family violence has a long and sordid history in Western civilization. During earlier human history wife beating was considered necessary to maintain family discipline.[171] The legal right of a husband to beat his wife was embedded in Western law and derived from ancient Roman customs. In Europe during the Middle Ages, husbands had the legal right to discipline their wives by physical means. Corporal punishment was intended to correct inappropriate female behavior but not when the husband was angry. During the Middle Ages it was legal for a husband to beat his wife with a stick the size of his thumb, using "moderate" blows. The expectation was that he would do "no bodily damage" during the beating.

In Puritan New England during colonial times, married women were becoming emancipated, and men were advised not to beat their wives unless they were attacked first. Other American religious groups also opposed wife beating, although it was still occurring. England passed laws making wife beating a crime in the 1850s after repeated urging by women's groups and enlightened men. Female neighbors and relatives of a battered wife would often take the victim in and protect her from harm by an abusive husband. Most historical complaints about wife beating concerned the degree of violence used rather than the fact of the beating itself. Family violence still occurs today, but it can be prosecuted if it is reported and the abused wife is willing to testify.

For centuries Catholic women had few options if they were trapped in abusive marriages, except annulment or separation, which were expensive and difficult to obtain for most people (although today annulments or separations are less costly).

Alternatives to Divorce

Prior to the easy availability of divorce, there were few options open to Catholic couples who had stopped loving each other. Under Catholic law the grounds for divorce were narrow or nonexistent. There was no way to obtain a divorce for cruelty or abuse, and the fee for an annulment was prohibitive for all but wealthy families, although that is no longer true. Currently, it's estimated that there are about 60,000 annulments granted annually in the U.S. The most common way of resolving a broken marriage under canon law was legal separation, whereby the parties lived in different houses, free from social and sexual obligations. An informal alternative to legal separation was desertion, when one spouse packed up his or her belongings and left the home in search of a new life.

An unusual alternative to divorce was the practice of husbands selling their wives to other men, a trend that appeared during the sixteenth century in many parts of Europe. Historians think the practice was uncommon, however.[172] Speculation is that wife sales were associated with adultery and that the wife was sold to the adulterer as compensation for damage to the husband and to make peace between the families. These wife sales took place in public and were apparently sanctioned by society and the church.

Perhaps the most drastic alternative to divorce was the French institution of *lettre de cachet de famille*, which was essentially an arrest warrant issued by the king that ordered a wife to be imprisoned for a certain interval.[173] Fathers and husbands used this method to imprison wastrel sons and immoral daughters or wives. A husband usually requested a *lettre de cachet* if his wife was violent, disregarded her marriage duties, or behaved in an immoral manner. Women sometimes requested a *lettre de cachet* if their husbands abused them, although with little success.

Divorce has become more available and frequent during this century.

Modern Divorce. Divorce rates began to climb at the beginning of the twentieth century and accelerated rapidly after 1960. Research into what caused the increased divorce rate found that psychological, economic, and social factors jointly affected the rate of divorce.[174] Historically, divorce was viewed as a form of social pathology, similar to suicide. Now, however, divorce is seen as a healthy corrective for an unhappy marriage. Several factors are associated with the current high divorce rate. Chief among them are the employment of women outside the home, no-fault divorce, marrying at a young age, unrealistic expectations about marriage, and relaxed social and moral attitudes toward divorce. Because over 70 percent of divorces are initiated by women, their influence on the rate of divorce has been given special attention.

There are various sources of information about why women file for divorce. One is by reviewing the petitions women file. We can also ask women directly why they file for divorce and interview them about the underlying reasons they are unhappy in their marital relationship. Frequent reasons given by women for divorce include physical or verbal abuse, financial problems, drinking, neglect of home and children, and loss of love. Men most often cite sexual incompatibility as the cause of divorce. Research scientists have searched for the psychological and social causes of divorce and believe that the major factors associated with divorce are immaturity, low social status, premarital pregnancy, differences in social and educational backgrounds, employment of the wife outside the home, and a history of divorce in the nuclear family, which indicates family experience or genetic factors may be involved in filing for divorce.

The high divorce rate among couples who marry young probably happens because immature persons marry for financial security, to escape a difficult family situation, or because of sexual attraction or pregnancy. Although we are not certain why, authors, social scientists, university faculty, lawyers, and judges have higher divorce rates than couples from lower socioeconomic classes, so social status alone can't be the major cause of divorce. Also, the direction of causality for many of these factors is not clear. For example, working women have a higher rate of divorce compared with women who stay at home. However, we don't know if the women who stay at home have a lower divorce rate because they are happy in their marriage or because they feel trapped financially and have no alternative way of earning a living. Another finding is that urban dwellers are more likely to divorce compared with persons who live in rural areas. Since more people live in cities today than a generation ago, that may partially explain the higher incidence of modern divorce. Economic factors also seem implicated in our higher modern divorce rates.

Economic Factors. Up until the last century, financial constraints kept many married couples together, even if the marriage was unhappy. Wives who had no work skills were forced to stay in unhappy marriages because they had no alternate means of support. Also, the traditional family was the basis of production prior to the age of industrialization. Husbands and wives worked on a farm or managed a small business to earn a living and raise their children. Following industrialization, it was easier for women to find work as teachers, nurses, secretaries, retail workers, or domestic servants. Employment outside the home gave women the ability to divorce and survive. During the 1920s working women were more apt to divorce and many stayed single longer than their mothers had. [175]

Many divorced women started working to support themselves, but there is evidence that employment of married women outside the home and recent changes in the laws governing custody of children, alimony, child support, and division of community assets have combined to increase the likelihood of divorce, especially among educated women.

Financial Incentives for Divorce. A major factor contributing to the current high divorce rate are laws conferring significant financial advantages on women after a divorce, including unequal division of marital property, alimony, child support, awarding women custody of children, and the opportunity to remarry after the divorce. Since women are often awarded alimony, custody of their children, and child support by the courts, these economic factors have created a significant incentive for women to divorce if they are unhappy. [176] Economic factors alone probably don't cause divorce, however. Instead, better economic opportunities raise women's expectations and made them less likely to tolerate marital unhappiness because they can divorce their husband and support themselves and their children by working, collecting child support, alimony payments, and receiving substantial marital assets at the time of divorce.

Child Custody and Divorce. An important legal change associated with a significant increase in divorce rates is who gets custody of the children. During the 19th century fathers generally received custody of children and courts could not grant a wife visitation rights without his consent. By the early 20th century, custody of children was more often awarded to the wife, especially if one of the children was under five years of age. [177] Today, women are more often successful in gaining custody of their children compared with men. Modern divorcing women often receive custody of their children, collect child support, get a larger portion of marital property, and collect alimony after they file for divorce. Divorce has also become socially acceptable and employment for women readily available, likely increasing the incidence of divorce. Personal factors also contribute to the high incidence of divorce in modern times.

Psychological Causes of Divorce. Some modern divorces are caused by differences in core values, addiction to alcohol or drugs, sexual incompatibility, financial issues, adultery, and abuse. [178] Value differences can create frustration and anger, especially if one partner tries to change his or her mate. Addiction creates serious problems if the addicted person won't get professional help. Some couples drift into a sexless marriage, leaving one or both spouses frustrated and unhappy. Financial issues can cause serious marital stress if one spouse wants to save money while the other wants to spend. If discussions about sex evolve into a power struggle or source of personal rejection, the marriage has probably broken down and divorce is likely.

Marital Arguments. All couples argue. However, if a couple has the same fight over and over without settling anything, their marriage is likely to be in trouble. If marital disputes disintegrate into shouting matches where the spouses go away angry and give each other the cold shoulder, that's a sign the marriage may have broken down. A healthy marriage requires love, trust, and respect. If spouses feel contempt for each other, the marriage is probably doomed. [179] Marital experts say the ratio of positive to negative interactions in a healthy marriage should be over five to one. Some couples simply drift apart and divorce, especially after the children leave home.

Drifting Apart. Feeling bored and disconnected can happen to couples after years of marriage. Once their children are gone, they've retired, stopped acquiring new interests, and settled into a dull routine, they can grow disinterested in each other and bored with their marriage. This can lead to adultery, separation, or divorce. Another cause of divorce is disagreements about how to raise the children.

Child-Rearing Disagreements. Marital difficulties can be caused by disagreements over child management. Different expectations about who should be responsible for child-rearing tasks such as night feedings, changing diapers, and disciplining the children can create problems. If the husband thinks his wife should be responsible for taking care of a baby and the house, that attitude is likely to create problems if his spouse wants help with child-rearing and house work. On the other hand, if the wife shifts most child care to her spouse, he will probably resent it. Women's changing expectations may also be a cause of the current high incidence of divorce,

Women's Expectations. Most divorces are initiated by women. One explanation is that women's expectations about marriage have increased over the years. Women want their partner to be their best friend and their marriage relationship to be a major source of happiness. When their spouse can't meet these heightened expectations, they divorce him. Many more women are educated, employed, financially independent, crave autonomy and can support themselves if they divorce.

Recent research suggests that the tendency to divorce may be inherited rather than learned in the family.

Is the Tendency to Divorce Inherited? It's well documented that children of divorced parents are more likely to divorce as adults. Until recently, it wasn't known if that association was the result of genetics or environment (are children of divorced parents more likely to divorce because they inherited a tendency to divorce or because of what they learned at home watching their parents get divorced?). A new study using data from Sweden looked at the marriages of over 19,000 adopted children, to see how often their marriages ended in divorce and whether their divorce rates were related to the divorce rates of their adopted or their biological parents. [180]

The researchers found that adopted children were 20 percent more likely to divorce if their biological parents divorced, but were no more likely to divorce if their adoptive parents split up, even after living through the divorce of their adopted parents as children. These same researchers also looked at biological and adopted children raised in the same homes. They found that children were 20 percent more likely to divorce if their biological parents had divorced, but the fact that their adoptive parents divorced made no difference in the divorce rate of the adopted children reared in the home where the divorce took place if the adopted children's biological parents had not divorced. These results strongly suggest that genetic factors are important in determining whether a couple divorces because living in the home of parents who divorce does not increase the likelihood of a child divorcing unless the child is genetically related to the divorcing parents.

Chapter 12

Conclusion

Modern couples marry when they fall in love and divorce when they become unhappy with each other. Only the ancient Incas and the Roman Catholic Church didn't allow divorce. No-fault divorce is available in most countries today, but for generations divorces were granted only on grounds of adultery, cruelty, desertion, or the commission of a serious crime. Adultery is the leading cause of divorce worldwide, with inability to produce children a close second, followed by physical abuse. Criticism, disrespect, jealousy, laziness, drunkenness, desertion, nonsupport, and bad temper also contribute to the high incidence of modern divorce.

Couples in a happy marriage aren't smarter, richer, or more sophisticated than their peers. Instead, happy couples find ways to keep negative feelings from destroying their relationships. Building and maintaining a happy marriage pays rich dividends, including a longer life, fewer illnesses, and more personal happiness.[181] Having a happy marriage is also good for children. Kids who grow up in high-conflict homes have elevated stress levels, are more often truant, suffer more significant bouts of depression, are more likely to be aggressive, experience more peer rejection, earn lower grades, and more often drop out of school than do children from happy homes. It's damaging to raise children in a high-conflict home, so staying together for the kids is not necessarily a good idea if you fight all the time in front of them. Getting divorced may also be damaging to children if it creates conflict, so what should a couple do if they aren't getting along? The best strategy is to work with a competent counselor before hiring a divorce lawyer.

There are several marriage types, but one consistently leads to divorce.

Types of Marriage

According to John Gottman, a nationally recognized American marriage expert, good marriages are based on friendship, mutual respect, and wanting to be together.[182] Happy couples go out of their way to stay connected, because they genuinely like each other and overlook trivial problems that make unhappy couples angry. Happy couples make sure their quarrels don't get out of hand, using signals to let each other know when it's time to stop fighting and make up. This can be as direct as saying, "I need a break," or as subtle as lowering their voices and laughing about the issue. Happily married couples work to repair any damage they may have done to their relationship during the argument. They are skilled at sending and receiving subtle repair signals to each other after a fight. Success in using repair attempts is a major factor in maintaining a happy marriage.

Based on years of research, Gottman categorized couples into five types: Conflict-Avoiding, Validating, Volatile, Hostile, and Hostile-Detached. Conflict-avoiding, validating, and volatile couples generally stay married, and hostile couples are unhappy but rarely divorce. On the other hand, hostile-detached couples often end their marriages with divorce. Consider the following characteristics of each marriage type:

Conflict Avoiders. These couples minimize attempts to persuade each other when they have a disagreement; they concentrate on areas of agreement. They avoid arguments, rarely ask each other for what they need, and feel their relationship is generally happy. These couples are independent of each other, have clear boundaries, and pursue separate interests. Conflict-avoiding couples can be caring in areas where they have common interests, and they generally maintain a positive-to-negative interaction ratio of five to one by avoiding topics on which they disagree.

Volatile Couples. Volatile couples are emotional about almost everything. When they disagree about something, they try to persuade their partner through discussion. Their disagreements are characterized by laughter, shared amusement, and humor. They love to debate and argue but don't insult or criticize each other. Volatile couples may express anger and insecurity during their discussions, but they stay connected and are honest in their communications. These couples rarely criticize each other, and they take steps to repair any damage they may have done to their relationship during an argument.

Validating Couples. These couples interact in a calm, relaxed way. They can be emotional but generally are relaxed and reasonable with each other. Validating couples emphasize supporting and understanding each other's points of view in a debate rather than arguing or getting angry. These couples may confront each other on certain limited topics, but avoid raising touchy issues over which they can become competitive and risk a power struggle. When they do become angry or competitive, they quickly recognize what is happening, calm themselves down, and compromise. When these couples argue, they only express mild emotions and quickly calm down. Their ratio of positive to negative interactions is above five to one.

Hostile Couples. Hostile couples interact like validating couples, except both partners are defensive during arguments. Generally, the husband is a validator and the wife an avoider. These couples criticize each other a great deal, using statements such as "you always" and "you never"; they whine a lot when they argue. During a disagreement they spend a lot of time going over their own positions and expend little effort trying to understand their spouses'. They may express contempt for each other during their debates, but they rarely damage the relationship to the point of a divorce.

Hostile-Detached Couples. These couples are locked in a continuous war. They are frustrated with each other most of the time and can't seem to find a way out of the continuing conflict. They criticize each other with a sense of detachment rather than honest emotion. Hostile-detached couples fight until one of them tries to back down, offers to compromise, or tries to withdraw from the argument and repair the damage—but the other spouse won't let him or her stop the fighting and make up. Instead, the other spouse keeps the cycle of anger and frustration alive until they eventually divorce. The other types of couples can regulate their negative emotions and repair any damage done to their relationship, but hostile–detached couples can't, so they eventually get a divorce.

A Happy Marriage

There are several things couples can do to make their marriage thrive.

Don't Try to Change Your Spouse. Maintaining a happy marriage is about loving, honoring, respecting, and supporting your spouse rather than trying to change him or her. Trying to change your spouse will do serious harm, so avoid it if you can.

Know Your Spouse. Staying connected gives a couple a solid foundation for maintaining a relationship. It's important for spouses to know about their partners' friends, stresses, dreams, beliefs, values, preferences, and worries. Also, spouses should know as much as they can about the successes, failures, and injuries experienced by their partners. To make a marriage succeed, it helps to understand how a mate deals with anger, depression, fear, and love.

Respect Each Other. Hostility and contempt cause couples to become defensive, while supportive and positive interactions cause couples to respect each other. Marital affection can't survive contempt, so make certain you respect your spouse and avoid criticizing or showing contempt. Try to maintain a positive-to-negative ratio of interactions above five to one.

Stay in Touch. Another secret for a happy marriage is to stay in touch with each other every day. Listen to your partner, and send a word of encouragement when he or she is having a bad day. Take time to do things with your spouse, and get together at the end of the day to find out how your spouse is feeling. Discuss when would be the best time to have a chat, and take turns talking about the day and how you feel about things. But don't give advice unless he or she asks for it.

Share Power. Neither spouse should control the partnership if you want to maintain a happy marriage. If your partner insists "my way or the highway," the marriage is in serious trouble. Sharing power doesn't mean you never express negative feelings or disagree. It's healthy to share anger and upset, but don't do serious damage to your relationship when you argue. Make certain you signal when to stop and repair any damage immediately.

Resolve Conflicts. Every marriage has conflict. Some disputes are minor and easy to resolve, while others are serious and can last for years. Examples of potential chronic problems include whether to have a baby, how much sex each spouse wants, who does the housework, what religion to teach the children, and how to discipline them. The key to living with chronic problems is to introduce humor, tolerance, and common sense when discussing them. Trying to understand each other's point of view and searching for a reasonable compromise will help resolve most disagreements.

Here are signs of a broken marriage.

A Broken Marriage

Being ambivalent about your marriage from time to time is normal, but take time to think before deciding to divorce—it's a big decision. Bad marriages are emotionally destructive, produce anxiety or depression, and tend to get worse rather than better. Consider the following signs that you might need to untie the knot.[183]

Power Imbalance. When one spouse is committed to making the marriage work while the other is not, that creates a power imbalance. If one spouse walks on eggshells and monitors every move to avoid upsetting his or her spouse, that signals a dysfunctional relationship. If either spouse is afraid to offer a suggestion or ask for something because it might cause a fight, and if any disagreement causes the other party to become critical, the marriage is in trouble.

Contempt. When spouses show contempt for each other, their marriage is in serious danger. Being critical and showing contempt leads to defensiveness and stonewalling. Most stonewalling is done by men, when they become flooded with emotions after their wives criticize them. When a couple has a disagreement, they can make efforts to repair the damage, or they can withdraw and sulk. Stonewalling or failed attempts at repair are bad signs for a marriage, because they indicate that the relationship is failing.

Blaming. Dysfunctional partners avoid accepting responsibility for their actions and claim someone else is always at fault. They misremember events, revise facts to make their own behavior perfect, and blame their spouses for all marital problems. Communication stops, they can't agree about what happened, old grievances recur, and they blame their spouses for their problems. Blaming is destructive for any marriage. Generally, both spouses share responsibility for marital problems; it's rarely all one spouse's fault.

Holding Grudges. Everyone gets their feelings hurt from time to time, but repeated hurts can produce bitterness and resentment. Spouses need to get over past hurts, or they will accumulate resentments and end up hating each other and filing for divorce. Forgiving lets each of you focus on the positive parts of a marriage and then get on with life and love. Don't deny hurt feelings, but try to let go of the anger, forgive the transgression, and repair the relationship.

Sexual Difficulties. Problems in the bedroom can destroy a marriage. Medical or emotional issues can be helped by treatment or counseling. It's estimated that about 15 percent of couples have sexless marriages. Sexless couples generally stay together because of children, money, or health issues. A sexless marriage is a serious problem if one spouse is unhappy with the arrangement. The average couple has sex approximately six times a month, but the frequency varies widely. If one spouse is not getting his or her sexual needs met, that's bad for the marriage; it can lead to adultery and divorce.

Adultery. Infidelity causes tremendous pain, and trust may be destroyed. Most of the time adultery signals the end of a marriage, unless the couple is willing to enter joint counseling and deal with the underlying problems that led to the adultery.

Endless Fighting. If a couple engages in the same fight over and over without settling anything, the marriage is in trouble. Arguments are inevitable in a marriage. It's the way the couple handles disagreements that makes the difference between a healthy marriage and a divorce. When disputes disintegrate into shouting matches in which the couple end up calling each other nasty names, go away angry, and give each other the cold shoulder for a week, the marriage is in trouble.

Family Violence. If there is shoving, hitting, or threats of violence in a home, the marriage is probably broken. The cycle of family violence begins with a single shove, followed by remorse. If the husband or wife lets it go, he or she risks starting a recurring cycle of violence, remorse, blame, and more violence.

Predominantly Negative Interactions. All couples have times when things go wrong and they are unhappy with each other. Experts say positive-to-negative interactions in a healthy marriage should occur in a ratio of about five to one. If a couple's interactions are mostly negative, that's a bad sign.

Deciding to Divorce

When considering a divorce, a couple should ask the following questions: Is the marriage sexless? Is it impossible to compromise? Is one spouse having an affair? Do they feel contempt for each other? Has marriage counseling failed? Is the relationship abusive? Are most interactions negative? Is it difficult to share feelings?[184] If the answer to several of these questions is yes, the marriage is likely headed for a divorce.

Getting a divorce is a big step, but few people know how to make that difficult decision. No one likes uncertainty, so many individuals rush into a divorce without thinking carefully about the alternatives. Procrastination, uncertainty, and second thoughts are natural when you are considering a divorce, because there is no guarantee you are making the right choice. Divorce has serious consequences. The key to making a good decision about divorce is to systematically review the pros and cons of a marriage, determine whether there is any likelihood of significant change, try marital counseling, and then decide to divorce based on the balance of pros and cons in your marriage.

Modern couples think marriage should offer happiness, personal growth, security, and sexual satisfaction. When these ideals aren't achieved, disappointed couples file for divorce and begin searching for new mates who will fulfill their needs. Unfortunately, divorce is damaging to children. Research shows that children from divorced families are more likely to suffer mental and emotional difficulties, do poorly in school, become delinquent or sexually promiscuous, and fail to develop their full potential compared with children from intact families.

Child-development authorities believe we should work to lower the divorce rate in order to avoid damaging children. Legal experts introduced the adversarial litigation process to weed out frivolous divorces and try to save children from the hazards of parental divorce. However, the adversarial legal system didn't lower the divorce rate significantly, and couples who go through a litigated divorce often end up hating each other and causing additional damage to their children after the divorce. Many modern couples who recognize that an adversarial divorce is destructive of families are opting for a collaborative divorce. How do these two systems of divorce work, and what are the pros and cons of each?

Collaborative or Litigated Divorce?

A collaborative divorce offers many benefits, including privacy, lower cost, transparency, client control, convenience, preservation of family relationships, protection of children, allowance of creative settlement solutions, and minimization of post-divorce conflicts.[185] The benefits of a litigated divorce include forced discovery, availability of a restraining order against family violence, and a court-ordered division of property and child custody arrangements if the parties are unable to settle their marital dispute. In a collaborative divorce, all communications and documents produced are confidential. In a litigated divorce, everything is public and subject to discovery. Professionals who want to protect their reputation; wealthy individuals with large estates they want to keep private; and anyone who has committed an indiscretion, such as adultery, will appreciate the benefit of keeping his or her personal life out of the courtroom by choosing a collaborative divorce.

The average cost of a collaborative divorce is lower than the average cost of a litigated divorce. Participants in the collaborative process agree to voluntarily produce all relevant financial and family information, which saves the expense of discovery disputes. In contrast, litigation attorneys hide documents and force the other side to submit formal discovery requests to uncover assets. A collaborative divorce is settled through interest-based negotiation, so clients control the outcome and don't turn their future over to a judge or jury, while a litigated divorce is controlled by attorneys and the court. The collaborative process helps divorcing couples learn to communicate and work together for the benefit of their children. A litigated divorce brings out the worst in people, makes them hate each other, and destroys their ability to co-parent their children after the divorce.

Children are never put in the middle of a collaborative divorce, while parents who are fighting over custody in a litigated divorce may force the children to talk with a judge in chambers or endure an invasive custody evaluation or social study. The collaborative process allows clients and their attorneys to reach creative settlements not generally available in court. Parties who participate in a collaborative divorce learn to respect each other and discover that fighting is not productive. Couples who opt for a collaborative divorce are able to co-parent effectively after the divorce. Many litigated divorces end up back in court to resolve disputes that could have been worked out between the parties if they had just been reasonable.

The Collaborative Process. During the first collaborative meeting, two attorneys, a financial professional, and a mental health professional explain the collaborative process, review expectations of conduct, discuss the collaborative family law participation agreement, and explore both spouses' goals and interests. The parties sign the participation agreement, and the financial professional lists the information needed for settlement. During the second joint meeting, the collaborative team and the parties review financial information, identify issues, create settlement options, and compare the expected outcomes of each option with the clients' stated goals and interests. The team eliminates any option that doesn't meet important goals and interests of both clients. During the next few collaborative meetings the team and parties negotiate a collaborative settlement agreement that meets the goals and interests of both parties. Finally, the parties sign an irrevocable collaborative settlement agreement summarizing the deal.

Following settlement, the attorneys jointly draft the Divorce Decree and Agreement Incident to Divorce. Once the closing documents are complete and signed, one attorney and his or her client will hold a prove-up, or final, hearing in court.

Litigation. The first step in a litigated divorce is to file an original petition, stating the grounds for divorce (usually incompatibility) or alleging fault (abuse, adultery, abandonment, fraud etc.). The divorce petition is served on the other spouse so that he or she has notice of the proceeding. The spouse who was served with the divorce petition must file a response. Next there is a hearing before a judge, who decides where the children will live while the divorce is ongoing, establish a visitation schedule until settlement or trial of the case, and determine how much temporary spousal and child support will be paid by one spouse to the other until the final divorce decree is entered.

Following the hearing for temporary orders, attorneys exchange requests for discovery and may schedule oral depositions of witnesses and the parties. Discovery fights can consume substantial time and money if the issues are complex and the parties resist producing financial documents. Often the attorneys must petition the court to settle discovery disputes that cannot be negotiated satisfactorily. These discovery fights cost money, generate animosity, and may not result in complete disclosure of all financial and personal information required for an equitable resolution of the dispute.

Once discovery is complete, the attorneys meet for settlement negotiations, or the court will order the parties to mediation in an effort to settle the dispute. About 80 percent of litigated cases settle before trial, following extensive discovery and trial preparation. If the parties disagree about custody, the court may order a social study to determine which parent should receive primary custody of the children. If the parties are unable to settle their dispute, the court will set the case for trial. At trial, both parties make opening statements, put on witnesses, introduce evidence, and make closing arguments. Then the court or jury decides the issues of the dispute, including who will have custody of the children, how the marital estate will be divided, the amount of child support to be paid, and what amount of spousal support, if any, is justified by the circumstances of the marriage. Finally, the attorneys will draft the Divorce Decree and Agreement Incident to Divorce to reflect the orders of the court.

Is Divorce Constructive?

The argument for no-fault divorce is that marriages break down for various reasons—including adultery, physical abuse, criminality, addiction, barrenness, or desertion—and forcing unhappy couples to stay married is not emotionally healthy for them or their children. On the other hand, studies show that litigated divorces are destructive to children. So, what's the answer? Should we restrict the availability of divorce to protect children or allow easy no-fault divorce to free unhappy couples from a broken marriage? There's no good solution for millions of unhappy couples with children who mistrust or hate each other. A legal separation is not satisfactory, because children would still be raised by a single parent, but if they stay together, the parents are likely to fight and harm their children as well.

A collaborative divorce can be a constructive way for a couple to end a broken marriage, divide their assets amicably, and co-parent their children effectively afterwards. A collaborative divorce helps spouses communicate effectively and treat each other reasonably following the divorce. However, divorces can be destructive if the couples choose an adversarial divorce, end up hating each other, fight all the time, and put their children in the middle of a brutal custody fight. Court-mandated custody arrangements can make it difficult for couples to cooperate; an adversarial divorce can cause bitterness and animosity between the parents, making it difficult for them to compromise.

In conclusion, the method of divorce you choose can determine whether the outcome is constructive (through a collaborative divorce) or destructive of the family and the children (through a litigated divorce).

Notes

1   Mike Vago, The Matriarchal Mosuo of China Enjoy Communal Living and "Walking Marriages," AV/AUX, February 5, 2017.

2   Helen Fisher, Anatomy of Love (New York: W. W. Norton and Co., 1992) 152-61.

3   Helen Fisher, Anatomy of Love (New York: W. W. Norton and Co., 1992) 37-58.

4   Kim Parker and Renee Stepler, As U.S. marriage rate hovers at 50%, education gap in marital status widens, Pew Research Center, September 14, 2017.

5   Duran Bell, Defining Marriage and Legitimacy, Current Anthropology 38 no. 2 (1997) 237-253,

6   Macaela Mackenzie, This Is The Average Age of Marriage Right Now, Women's Health, March 26, 2018.

7   Robert H. Shmerling, The health advantages of marriage, Harvard Health Publishing, Harvard Medical School, November 30, 2016.

8   Andy Coghlan, Darwin dynasty's ill health blamed on inbreeding, New Scientist, Daily News, Mary 3, 2010.

9   Tessa Berenson, Here's How China's One-Child Policy Started in The First Place, Time, October 29, 2015.

10 Andrew J. Cherlin, Frank F. Furstenberg, P. Lindsey Chase-Lansdale, and Kathleen E. Kiernan, Longitudinal Studies of Effect of Divorce on Children in Great Britain and the United States, Science no. 252 (June 7, 1991) 1386-89.

11 David Gale and Lloyd Shapley, College Admissions and the Stability of Marriage, The American Mathematical Monthly 69, no. 1 (January 1962) 9-15.

12 Judith C. Areen, Uncovering the Reformation Roots of American Marriage and Divorce Law, 26 Yale Journal of Law and Feminism, 126 (2014) 29-89.

13 Divorce Rate by Country: The World's 10 Most and Least Divorced Nations, Family Law, September 29, 2017.

14 Gary Goodpaster, On the Theory of American Adversary Criminal Trial, Journal of Criminal Law and Criminology, 78 no. 1 (Spring 1987) 118-54.

15 Peter T. Leeson, Trial by Battle, <u>Journal of Legal Analysis</u>, 3 no. 1 (Spring 2011) 341-75.

16 John Thibaut and Laurens Walker, A Theory of Procedure, 66 <u>California Law Review</u> (1978) 541

17 Kim Munsinger (Ed), <u>Collaborative Law-Start to Finish</u> (Austin: Texas Bar Books, 2014).

18 Kansas State University, What are the Advantages of Mediation? <u>Human Capital Services</u>, May 05, 2018.

19 Kim Munsinger (Ed), <u>Collaborative Law-Start to Finish</u> (Austin: Texas Bar Books 2014).

20 Mike Vago, The Matriarchal Mosuo of China Enjoy Communal Living and "Walking Marriages," <u>AV/AUX</u>, February 5, 2017.

21 Henry V. Sattler, Sacramental Grace in Marriage, <u>National Catholic Conference on Family Life</u>, 1956 87-94.

22 Matt Baume, What's the Real Definition of "Traditional Marriage?" <u>Huffington Post</u>, June 26, 2016.

23 Kristyn Bellman, What Bonobos Can Teach Us About Sex, Society and Ourselves, <u>the dodo</u>, September 11, 2014.

24 Jenna Goudreau, Why Men And Women Get Married, <u>Forbes</u>, May 27, 2010.

25 Beth A. Jerskey, Matthew S. Panizzon, Kristen C. Jacobson, Michael C. Neale, Michael D. Grant, Mark Schultz, Seth A. Eisen, Ming T. Tsuang, and Michael J. Lyons, Marriage and Divorce: A Genetic Prospective, <u>Personality and Individual Differences</u>, 49 no. 5 (October 1, 2010) 473-78.

26 Beth A. Jerskey, Matthew S. Panizzon, Kristen C. Jacobson, Michael C. Neale, Michael D. Grant, Mark Schultz, Seth A. Eisen, Ming T. Tsuang, and Michael J. Lyons, Marriage and Divorce: A Genetic Prospective, <u>Personality and Individual Differences</u>, 49 no. 5 (October 1, 2010) 473-78.

27 Emily Dugan, "Bridenapping": A growing hidden crime, <u>Independent</u>, October 9, 2011.

28 Bride-Price, <u>International Encyclopedia of Marriage and Family.com</u>, 2003.

29 Marriage in Ancient Greece, <u>Greek Data</u>, February 2019.

30 Jacob Marries Leah and Rachel, <u>Bible</u>, 29: 14b-30.

31 Chen Yueyang, Ancient bride-price custom unsuited to modern China, <u>Global Times</u>, August 7, 2014.

32 The Origin of Wedding Rings and Why They're Worn on the 4th Finger of the Left Hand, <u>DanforthDiamond.com</u>, September 27, 2010.

33 Laura Betzig, Roman monogamy, <u>Ethology and Sociobiology</u>, 13 (September-November 1992) 351-83.

34 Kristen Droesch, Wedding Traditions From Around the World, <u>Huffington Post</u>, September 29, 2013.

35   Cosmo Luce, Here's The Best Time to Get Married, According to Moon Phases, <u>Elite Daily</u>, January 19, 2018.

36   BBC History Magazine, Love and Marriage in Medieval England, <u>History Extra</u>, February 13, 2019.

37   D'Vera Cohn, Jeffrey S. Passel, Wendy Wang, and Gretchen Livingston, Barely Half of U.S. Adults Are Married—A Record Low, <u>Pew Research Center</u>, December 14, 2011.

38   Nigel Barber, The Three Reasons for Polygamy, <u>Psychology Today</u>, October 23, 2012.

39   Anastasia J. Gage-Brandon, The Polygyny-Divorce Relationship: A Case Study of Nigeria, <u>Journal of Marriage and The Family</u>, 54, no. 2 (1992) 285-92.

40   John D. Clare, Download Native American Marriage &Divorce Facts & Information, <u>School History</u>, 2018.

41   Wendy McElroy, The Free Love Movement and Radical Individualism, <u>Libertarian Enterprise</u>. 19 no. 1 (1996).

42   J. David Hacker, Libra Hilde, and James Holland Jones, The Effect of the Civil War on Southern Marriage Patterns, <u>Journal of Southern History</u>, 76 no. 1 (2010) 39-70.

43   Hannah Devlin, Early men and women were equal, say scientists, <u>The Guardian</u>, May 14, 2015.

44   Matthew Philips, Did Gender Inequality Start with the Plow? <u>Freakonomics</u>, June 23, 2011.

45   Where does social inequality come from? Hunter-Gatherer to Agriculture, <u>UCL Public Policy Analysis</u>, January 31, 2015.

46   Dasia Echevarria, The Double Standards of Gender in Society, <u>Odyssey</u>, May 8, 2017.

47   Susan C. Rogers, female forms of power and the myth of male dominance: a model of female/male interaction in peasant society, <u>American Ethnologist</u> (1975) 727-56.

48   Jefferson M. Fish, Arranged Marriages, <u>Psychology Today</u>, April 27, 2010.

49   Jefferson M. Fish, Arranged Marriages, <u>Psychology Today</u>, April 27, 2010.

50   Kimberly F. Schutte, <u>Marrying by the Numbers: Marriage Patterns of Aristocratic British Women,</u> Ph.D. Dissertation, University of Kansas (April 18, 2011) 1485-2000.

51   Ancient Egypt Online, <u>Fact about Marriage in Ancient Egypt,</u> December 20, 2018.

52   Simon Newman, Marriage in the Middle Ages, <u>The Finer Times</u>, 2008-18.

53   Office of the High Commissioner-United Nations Human Rights, <u>Women's economic, social and cultural rights.</u>

54   Roy Sanchari, Empowering women? Inheritance rights, female education and dowry payments in India, <u>Journal of Developmental Economics</u>, 114 (May 2015) 233-51.

55   The Country House Reader, <u>The Servant Hierarchy</u>, December 19, 2013.

56   The Editors of Encyclopaedia Britannica, Primogeniture and ultimogeniture. <u>Law</u>

57   Zeng Yi, <u>China-Living Arrangements And Family Support</u>, 2017.

58   Global Education Monitoring, Education leading for gender equality, <u>World Education Blog</u>, October 4, 2016.

59   Catalyst, Women in the Workforce: India, <u>Knowledge Center</u>, July 11, 2018.

60   Michelle Singletary, Being married has a lot to do with economic success, scholars say, <u>The Washington Post</u>, October 28, 2014.

61   Betty Friedan, <u>The Feminine Mystique</u> (New York: W. W. Norton & Co., 1963).

62   Libby Gail, <u>Stay-At-Home Dads: The Essential Guide to Creating the New Family</u> (New York: Penguin Group, 2001)

63   Isabella Steger, People don't want to get married in South Korea anymore, <u>Quartz</u>, March 18, 2018.

64   John Phelan, Harvard Study: "Gender Wage Gap" Explained Entirely by Work Choices of Men and Women, <u>Foundation for Economic Education</u>. December 10, 2018.

65   Valentin Bolotnyy and Natalia Emanuel, <u>Why Do Women Earn Less Than Men? Evidence from Bus and Train Operators</u>, Working Paper, November 28, 2018.

66   Wendy Johnson, Matt McGue, Robert F. Krueger, and Thomas J. Bouchard, Jr., Marriage and personality: A genetic analysis, <u>Journal of Personality and Social Psychology</u>, 86 no. 2 (2004) 285-94.

67   Wendy Johnson, Matt McGue, Robert F. Krueger, and Thomas J. Bouchard, Jr., Marriage and personality: A genetic analysis, <u>Journal of Personality and Social Psychology</u>, 86 No. 2 (2004) 285-94.

68   Alain Testart, The Significance of Food Storage among Hunter-Gatherers: Residence Patterns, Population Densities, and Social Inequalities, <u>Current Anthropology</u>, 2, no. 5 (1982) 523-37.

69   Alain Testart, The Significance of Food Storage among Hunter-Gatherers: Residence Patterns, Population Densities, and Social Inequalities, <u>Current Anthropology</u>, 2 no. 5 (1982) 523-37.

70   Alain Testart, The Significance of Food Storage among Hunter-Gatherers: Residence Patterns, Population Densities, and Social Inequalities, <u>Current Anthropology</u>, 2 no. 5 (1982) 523-37.

71 Jerry Moore, "Claude Levi-Strauss: Structuralism", in, <u>Visions of Culture: An Introduction to Anthropological Theories and Theorists.</u> (Walnut Creek, California: Altamira, 2009) 231-247.

72 Trishna Buch, Arranged Marriages: They're Not as Unfortunate as You Think, <u>The Cougar,</u> April 3, 2015.

73 Omiai: The Culture of Arranged marriage in Japan, <u>Japan Information.</u> December 11, 2015.

74 Neel Burton, The Pros and Cons of Polygamy, <u>Psychology Today</u>, January 4, 2018.

75 Hayyim Schauss, Ancient Jewish Marriage, <u>Jewish Learning</u>.

76 United States Conference of Catholic Bishops, <u>Annulment</u>, 2019.

77 A Brief History of Celibacy in the Catholic Church, <u>Future Church.</u>

78 Jim Blackburn, What Are Grounds for Annulment? <u>Pro-Life Answers,</u> January 1, 2016.

79 Joe Carter, 9 Things You Should Know About the Council of Trent, <u>The Gospel Foundations</u>, December 5, 2013.

80 Editors of the Encyclopaedia Britannica, Reformation, <u>Encyclopaedia Britannica.</u>

81 Huda, Islamic Marriage and Involvement of Friends and Family, <u>Thought Co.</u>, October 13, 2017.

82 John Gottman and Nan Silber, What Makes Marriage Work? <u>Psychology Today</u>, March 1, 1994.

83 Douglas LaBier, Women Initiate Divorce Much More Than Men, Here's Why, <u>Psychology Today</u>, August 28, 2015.

84 Kathy Caprino, What Is Feminism, And Why Do So Many Women and Men Hate It? <u>Forbes</u>, March 8, 2017.

85 The Pill and the Sexual Revolution, <u>American Experience</u>.

86 Feminists sit-in at Ladies Home Journal to protest the magazine's depiction of women, <u>Global Nonviolent Action Database</u>. March 18,1970.

87 Neel Burton, A Feminist Critique of Marriage, <u>Psychology Today</u>, August 4, 2017.

88 Betty Friedan, <u>The Feminine Mystique</u> (New York, W. W. Norton & Co., 1963).

89 Germaine Greer, <u>The Female Eunuch</u> (London, Paladin, 1970) 11-22.

90 Robert M. Thomas, Jr. Jessie Bernard, 93: Ideas Inspired Feminists, <u>New York Times</u>, October 11, 1996.

91 Marabel Morgan, <u>The Total Woman</u> (Old Tappan, N.J.: Revell, 1973).

92 Patricia O'Brien, <u>Staying Together: Marriages That Work</u> (New York: Random House, 1977).

93 Sharon Bond, Couple and Family Therapy: The Evolution of the Profession with Social Work at its Core, <u>Interventions</u>. 131 (2009) 128-38.

94   Millennials, <u>San Antonio Express News</u>, January 2, 2019.
95   William R. Greer, The Changing Women's Marriage Market, <u>The New York Times</u>, February 22, 1986.
96   Mary Blair-Loy, <u>Competing Devotions: Career and Family Among Women Executives</u> (Cambridge, Mass.: Harvard University Press, 2003) 71-73.
97   Elizabeth Matsangou, For richer for poorer: The economics of marriage, <u>World Finance</u>, October 28, 2017.
98   Margaret Talbot, The Price of Divorce, <u>The New York Times</u>, October 1, 2000.
99   Love and Marriage: A History that Challenges the Notion of "Traditional Marriage," <u>Salt Lake Tribune</u>, February 14, 2014.
100   Rebecca Tushnet, Rules of Engagement, <u>Yale Law Journal</u>, 107 (1998) 1-5.
101   Rudy A. Jaworski, <u>Forty Years On, No-Fault Divorce Faces Scrutiny,</u> January 1, 2010.
102   <u>GI Bill: Veterans Benefits Administration,</u> U.S. Department of Veterans Affairs.
103   Michael Chang, Why did the divorce rate increase after World War 2? <u>Quora</u>, May 6, 2018.
104   Sigmund Freud, <u>The Psychopathology of Everyday Life</u> (New York: Penguin Classics, 2003).
105   Ana Swanson, 144 years of marriage and divorce in the United States, in one chart, <u>The Washington Post</u>, June 23, 2015.
106   Stephanie Coontz, <u>Marriage, a History: How Love Conquered Marriage</u> (New York: Penguin Books, 2005).
107   Mirah Riben, The Perversion of American Birth Certificates, <u>Huffington Post</u>. December 6, 2017
108   Institute of Human Development, Annual Report, <u>Human Development, Institute of</u>. Berkeley, 1962.
109   The 1960s, <u>History,</u> 2019.
110   Kenneth T. Walsh, The 1960s: A Decade of Change for Women, <u>U.S. News & World Report</u>, March 12, 2010.
111   Aziz Ansari and Eric Klinenberg, How to Make Online Dating Work, <u>The New York Times</u>, June 13, 2015.
112   Kathy McCoy, 7 Surprising Facts About Gray Divorce, <u>Psychology Today</u>, September 25, 2018
113   Sheri Stritof, Cohabiting Statistics, <u>The Spruce</u>, December 13, 2018.
114   Tasha Wibawa, The Philippines is one of two countries where divorce is illegal, trapping women in marriages. <u>ABC News</u>, October 8, 2018.
115   Camille W. Cook, Chinese Family Law: A Potential Statutory Revolution, 9 <u>Loyola of Los Angeles International and Comparative Law Review,</u> 63, (September 1, 1986).
116   Divorce in China, <u>Facts and Details</u>.

117 Stanford University News Service, <u>Ancient Romans led the way in no-fault divorce,</u> December 3, 1991.

118 John Trigilio, Jr. and Kenneth Brighenti, <u>The Twelve Articles of Catholic Faith--Catholicism for Dummies, Cheat Sheet, 3rd Ed.</u> (Chicago: IDG Books, 2017).

119 Christopher Phu, Sacred Kingship, <u>Christian History Institute,</u> 108, (2014).

120 The Earl of Bothwell and Mary Queen of Scots, Scotland's Mary, <u>Word Press.</u>

121 History.com Editors, Martin Luther and the 95 Theses, <u>History,</u> January 14, 2019.

122 Mary Hallward-Driemeier, Tzzeen Hasan and Anca Bogdana Rusu, Women's Legal Rights Over 50 Years: What Is the Impact of Reform? <u>Open Knowledge Forum,</u> 2013.

123 Editors of the Encyclopaedia Britannica, The Napoleonic Code, <u>Encyclopaedia Britannica.</u>

124 Anthony C. Moses, The Development of Common Law in England from 1066 to the 19th Century, <u>Pleaders,</u> April 9, 2018.

125 U.K. Parliament, <u>Obtaining a Divorce,</u> www.parliament.uk.

126 1857-<u>Matrimonial Causes Act 1857,</u> Perfar.

127 Judith Areen, Uncovering the Reformation Roots of American Marriage and Divorce Law, <u>Yale Journal of Law & Feminism,</u> Volume 26, 1, Article 3, 2014.

128 Reuven P. Bulka, The Wife's Grounds for Divorce, <u>Chabad.org.</u>

129 Why Catholic Priests Practice Celibacy, <u>The Economist,</u> March 23, 2017.

130 The United States Conference of Catholic Bishops, Annulment. <u>UCCCB.</u>

131 The United States Conference of Catholic Bishops, Annulment. <u>UCCCB.</u>

132 <u>Collins English Dictionary, Definition of Judicial Separation</u> (New York: Harper Collins, 1979).

133 Joe Carter, 9 Things You Should Know About the Council of Trent, <u>The Gospel Coalition,</u> December 5, 2013.

134 Thomas More, <u>Utopia,</u> Global Gray free PDF, 1551.

135 Bethany Blankley, How Protestantism Redefined Marriage, <u>Huffington Post,</u> July 15, 2012.

136 Khula, <u>Islamic Sharia Council.</u>

137 Natalie Shoemaker, Divorce Wasn't Considered Taboo Among 17th Century, New World Puritans, <u>Big Think.com,</u> January 6, 2015.

138 Troy L. Harris, ed., Studies in Canon Law and Common Law in Honor of R.H. Helmholz, (Berkeley, Ca.: The Robbins Collection), Hugo Grotius and the Natural Law of Marriage: A Case Study of Harmonizing Confessional Differences in Early Modern Europe, <u>Emory Legal Studies Research Paper</u> (January 13, 2017) 26 pages.

[139] Robert S. Walker, Kim R. Hill, Mark V. Flinn and Ryan E. Ellsworth, Evolutionary History of Hunter-Gatherer Marriage Practices, PLoS One, April 27, 2011.

[140] Rebecca Sear and Ruth Mace, Who keeps children alive? A review of the effect of kin on child survival, LSE Research Online, Evolution and Human Behavior, 29 no. 1 (2008) 1-18.

[141] Editors of the Encyclopaedia Britannica, Code of Hammurabi, Encyclopaedia Britannica,

[142] Marriage and Divorce in Mesopotamia, Facts and Details

[143] Yoel Shiloh, "For She Was Barren": Infertility as Grounds for Divorce, Bar-Ilan University's Parashat Hashavua Study Center, Parashat Toledot, December 4, 2005.

[144] Maurice Lamm, The Jewish Marriage Contract (Ketubah), Chabad ORG.

[145] Constanca Costa, Marriage & Divorce in Ancient Greece, Prezi, November 20, 2014.

[146] Stanford University News Service, Ancient Romans led the way in no-fault divorce, Stanford University, December 3, 1991.

[147] Editors of the Encyclopaedia Britannica, Code of Justinian, Encyclopaedia Britannica.

[148] Editors of the Encyclopaedia Britannica, Reformation, Encyclopaedia Britannica.

[149] 1857-Matrimonial Causes Act 1857, Parfar.

[150] Editors of the Encyclopaedia Britannica, Napoleonic Code, Encyclopaedia Britannica.

[151] Hendrik A. Hartog, Marital Exits and Marital Expectations in Nineteenth Century America, Scholarship @ Georgetown Law, 1991.

[152] Lee Strauss, Marriage and Divorce in the 1920s, Lee Strauss.com, April 27, 2018.

[153] Ana Swanson, 144 years of marriage and divorce in the United States, in one chart, The Washington Post, June 23, 2015.

[154] Rebecca Clifford-Cruz and Delen Goldberg, Why Sin City is the wedding mecca and divorce capital of the country, Law Vegas Sun, June 15, 2015.

[155] Jeremy Byellin, Today in 1969: California Passes the First No-Fault Divorce Law in the U.S., Legal Solutions Blog, September 4, 2015.

[156] Stephanie Coontz, Divorce, No-Fault Style, The New York Times, June 16, 2010.

[157] Wendy McElroy, The Economics of Marriage and Divorce, Foundation for Economic Education, July 8, 2014.

[158] Margareth Lanzinger, Marriage, Marriage Contracts and Legal Cultures, Anneles De Demographie Historique, 121 no. 1 (2011) 69-97.

159   Serena Goldring, Gender Roles in the Industrial Society, Prezi, October 31, 2013.

160   Melanie Notkin, The "Career Woman" Myth, Psychology Today, February 17, 2012.

161   Gad Saad, Do Men or Women File for Divorce More Often? Psychology Today, November 14, 2013.

162   Sam Jenkinson, What are the Economic Consequences of Divorce? An income study focusing on divorced men and women in the UK 1992-2008, Master's Thesis, Lund University, June 2015.

163   How Much Does Divorce Cost in the USA. Divorce Statistics.

164   J. M. Ansen, Community Property States vs. Common Law, Asset Protection Plan.

165   Texas Family Code, Title 1, Chapter 7, April 7, 1997.

166   Ken Paxton, Attorney General of Texas, Child Support in Texas, Office of the Attorney General of Texas.

167   Leticia Summers, 5 Surprisingly Common Causes of Divorce, Divorce Magazine.com, August 17, 2018.

168   Leticia Summers, 5 Surprisingly common Causes of Divorce, Divorce Magazine.com, August 17, 2018.

169   Sheila Gregoire, Household Responsibilities: Negotiating with your spouse, Focus on the Family, 2013.

170   Shellie Warren, 10 Most Common Reasons for Divorce, Marriage.com. December 11, 2018.

171   Jone Johnson Lewis, Rule of Thumb Origin and the Legality of Wife-Beating, Thought Co, January 7, 2019.

172   Goran Blazeski, The strange English custom of wife selling, The Vintage News, November 20, 2016.

173   Editors of the Encyclopaedia Britannica, Lettre de cachet, Encyclopaedia Britannica.

174   Shellie Warren, 10 Most Common Reasons for Divorce, Marriage.com. December 11, 2018.

175   Lee Strauss, Marriage & Divorce in the 1920s, Lee Strauss.com, April 27, 2018.

176   Chester G. Vernier and John B. Hurlbut, The Historical Background of Alimony Law and Its Present Statutory Structure, Law and Contemporary Problems.

177   Ralph J. Podell, Harry F. Peck, and Curry First, Custody—To Which Parent? Marquette Law Review, 56 no. 1 (1972).

178   Shellie Warren, 10 Most Common Reasons for Divorce, Marriage.com. December 11, 2018.

179   Eva Van Prooven, This One Thing is the Biggest Predictor of Divorce, The Gottman Institute, August 25, 2017.

[180] Amanda MacMillan, Is Divorce Hereditary? Here's How Your Genes May Be Partially to Blame, <u>Health</u>, October 5, 2017.

[181] Glenn Stanton, Hidden Benefits of Marriage, <u>Focus on the Family</u>, 2012.

[182] Diane Coutu, Making Relationships Work, <u>Harvard Business Review</u>, December 2007.

[183] Denise Schipani, Lenore Skomal, and Nicol Natale, Should I Get a Divorce? Experts Say These Are the Signs That you Should, <u>Woman's Day,</u> January 10, 2019.

[184] Denise Schipani, Lenore Skomal, and Nicol Natale, Should I Get a Divorce? Experts Say These Are the Signs That you Should, <u>Woman's Day,</u> January 10, 2019.

[185] Russell J. Frank, The Pros and Cons of The Collaborative Divorce Process, <u>Divorce Magazine.com</u>. February 2, 2017.

Printed in the United States
By Bookmasters